Struck Out

STRUCT OUT

Why Employment Tribunals Fail Workers and What Can be Done

David Renton

First published 2012 by Pluto Press
345 Archway Road, London N6 5AA

www.plutobooks.com

Distributed in the United States of America exclusively by
Palgrave Macmillan, a division of St. Martin's Press LLC,
175 Fifth Avenue, New York, NY 10010

British Library Cataloguing in Publication Data
A catalogue record for this book is available from the British Library

ISBN 978 0 7453 3256 7 Hardback
ISBN 978 0 7453 3255 0 Paperback

Library of Congress Cataloging in Publication Data applied for

This book is printed on paper suitable for recycling and made from fully managed and sustained forest sources. Logging, pulping and manufacturing processes are expected to conform to the environmental standards of the country of origin.

10 9 8 7 6 5 4 3 2 1

Designed and produced for Pluto Press by Chase Publishing Services Ltd
Typeset from disk by Stanford DTP Services, Northampton, England
Simultaneously printed digitally by CPI Antony Rowe, Chippenham, UK and Edwards Bros in the United States of America

Contents

List of Tables

Preface

Several years ago,[1] I found myself in an Employment Tribunal waiting room. In a corner of the room, I noticed an old friend, a man I had seen just once or twice in the past ten years. My friend is a barrister, although not an employment law specialist. You are more likely to see him at work in the High Court or the Court of Appeal. He was speaking hurriedly to a client. I tried to catch my friend's eye but he was too busy to notice me. Some months later, we began to correspond after what had been a long gap. I mentioned to him the occasion on which we had nearly met. 'I do hate Employment Tribunals', he wrote back, 'they are such unhappy places.' With that casual phrase, my friend had supplied the theme of this book.

My subject is the disparity between the ambitions of the Tribunal claimant who brings a claim complaining about injustice at work, and the outcome which that claimant is likely to receive from even a favourable Tribunal judgment, which almost always offers the claimant no remedy other than financial compensation usually of a modest amount. This, it follows, is a project of multiple explanation. I want claimants, trade unionists, and all the other non-lawyers who have an interest in fair relationships at work to understand *why* it is that the remedies are limited to money, and *why* it is that the remedies are low. As for lawyers, I want more of us to grasp, in a way that most of us do not, how rare it is for our priorities to match our clients'.

I want to explain to claimants and their advisers why the Tribunal is often an inadequate forum for the address of grievances. I want both groups to understand that if they have lost, it may not be *their fault*. I write above all with the intention of persuading workers that other strategies for resolving wrongs, including raising complaints collectively through their unions, often achieve better results.

Although there is much law in this book, and I have made every effort to make it as accurate as possible, this is by no means a textbook. Its central message is that where the law creates problems, the answers are outside the law. This is as much a work of politics, history and sociology, as a book of law.

My intention in writing this book has been to encourage discussion, in particular among trade unionists, claimants' representatives, workers themselves and those sympathetic to workers' claims. While I have discussed its contents with many friends and colleagues, this book is intended above all to persuade others to take sides. It is not the product of any party line. And if any reader, on reading all of it, finds that they agree with the entire argument, they have missed the point. This book is intended to mark the beginning and not the end of a debate.

* * *

At the outset of the book, I need to explain some of the language I use. The Tribunals (originally 'Industrial Tribunals') were established by the Industrial Training Act 1964, to resolve disputes between employers and government concerning the industrial training levy. Their functions were expanded by the Industrial Relations Act 1971, under which they acquired jurisdiction to hear complaints of unfair dismissal. Their powers have increased widely since. The Tribunals were renamed Employment Tribunals by section 1 of the Employment Rights (Dispute Resolution) Act 1998. To avoid complication, and except where quoting from other sources, this book refers to both pre- and post-1998 Tribunals as 'Employment Tribunals'.

In law, everyone who works is a 'worker', while the word 'employee' is restricted to a smaller group of people who work under an employment contract. An employment contract is a contract of subordination (in the nineteenth century, the law termed the people we now call employees 'servants'). A management consultant may be a worker; they are probably not an employee. The importance of this distinction is set out in Chapter 3, on agency workers; an important example of a kind of worker who is generally found by the courts *not* to be an employee.

The focus of this book is on the Employment Tribunal and to a lesser extent the Employment Appeal Tribunal (EAT) at which appeals from the Tribunal are heard. The Employment Tribunal is required to follow any relevant decisions of the EAT. All decisions of the EAT are available on its website, and some important decisions of the EAT are also published in law reports, such as the Industrial Cases Report (ICR) and the Industrial Law Reports (IRLR). Decisions of the Employment Tribunal do not bind another Tribunal, and for this reason they are not published or generally available, although they can be ordered from the Employment Tribunal Field Support Office in Bury St Edmunds,[2] on payment of a £10 fee. Sometimes a winning party will publicise the text of a favourable decision; as happened, for example, in 2010 and 2011 when several construction workers brought blacklisting claims in the Tribunal, and Tribunal decisions (sometimes favourable to the workers, sometimes to the employers) were circulated by both sides. Because Tribunal decisions are generally unavailable, most cases cited in this book are appeals.

Employment Tribunals are by no means the only court that can hear a worker's complaint. If the complaint concerns an injury at work, the claim will be heard in the civil court system; that is, in a county court or the High Court, depending on the complexity of the case and its financial value. Tribunals can hear some damages claims, for example, where they are part of a discrimination claim (as when a worker complains of suffering discriminatory harassment which may have caused her to suffer a deterioration in her mental health). Unlike the civil courts, Tribunals can hear a case only if statute specifically allows the claim to be heard in the Tribunal. In the ordinary civil courts, there are several types of claim which are typically brought by workers, for example, breach of contract claims. But there are other types of claim which are typically brought by employers, for example, where the employer seeks an 'injunction' (that is, an order) to prevent a former employee from competing with him.

Where an employee brings a breach of contract claim in the Tribunal, the employer can 'counter-claim', that is, seek damages in return.[3] But this is a highly unusual state of affairs. In every other case, the only person bringing a claim is a worker, and she is termed the 'claimant'. The employer, defending the claim, is the 'respondent'. In practice, therefore, every reference in this book to a claimant or to claimants is a reference to a worker or to workers; and every reference to a respondent or to respondents is a reference to an employer or to employers.

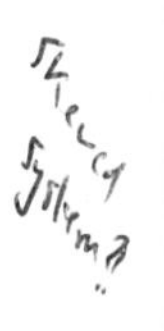

Appeals from the Employment Tribunal are heard by the Employment Appeal Tribunal. But even the EAT is not the final court to which an appeal may be taken. Appeals from the EAT are heard by the Court of Appeal, and appeals from that court by the Supreme Court.[4] Any Tribunal, as well as the Employment Appeal Tribunal, the Court of Appeal and the Supreme Court, may refer a case to the European Court of Justice (the ECJ, the highest court of the European Community) in a case which concerns European law. Where the case concerns human rights, on exhaustion of all domestic remedies, an applicant may take their case to the European

Court of Human Rights (ECHR). I say very little about any of these higher courts in this book, for the reason that from the point of view of the ordinary employment lawyer, they are exotic beasts, almost never encountered. Only one in 20 of all fully heard Employment Tribunal claims is appealed, and an even smaller proportion make it through to a full hearing at the Employment Appeal Tribunal. Barely a handful of UK employment cases make it to the ECJ or ECHR in any year.

That is not to say that all these other courts are irrelevant. One theme of this book is that the custom and practice of decision making in the Employment Tribunal are over-determined by ways of doing law developed in the 'common law', that is, in the very different world of the civil courts. But the subject of this book is the Tribunal and it is always to the Tribunal that the discussion returns.

* * *

Throughout this book, there is a constant contrast between litigation (the practice of resolving individual employment disputes in the courts) and negotiation (the habit of resolving disputes through agreement in the workplace). Some of my readers, I am aware, will be experienced workplace representatives. Others, including students, may have limited experience of workplace negotiation. Others still may be lawyers or claimants, and may fit somewhere in between. In the next section of this preface, therefore, I set out in some details how workplace negotiation can work.

The most important mechanism for negotiating workplace rights in the UK today is negotiation ('collective bargaining') between managers and unions. Around 7 million workers are members of unions, which is equivalent to just over one in four of all workers.[5] The number of trade unionists in the UK is, on any comparison, high. There are more members of unions than there are of any other type of voluntary organisation in the country, including churches and sports groups. The proportion of workers who are union members is higher here than in Greece, Germany, France, or Spain. The number of trade unionists has fallen in the past 30 years, from a peak of around 13 million in 1979, but to over-emphasise this decline would be misleading. There are more trade unionists in Britain today than there were at the times when unions were at their most visible in national life; such as during the labour unrest of 1911–14 or the General Strike of 1926.[6]

Trade union representation affects a much wider category of workers than just members of trade unions. Where a union is recognised, it will negotiate on behalf of all the workers in any grade, and where it makes an agreement with the employer (for example, over pay), the agreement will determine the terms under which all the workers are employed, not just the members of the union. It is not unusual for a union to be recognised despite less than half the employees in any grade being its members. Indeed, where relations are settled between an employer and a union, there is no incentive for non-members to join. Whether workers join the union or not, negotiations will continue, and they personally will be bound by the results. Where non-members of a recognised union (or even indeed members of that union) are dissatisfied with an agreement negotiated by the union on their behalf, the courts will uphold the agreement against their complaints.[7]

So, although only a quarter of all workers are members of unions, a third of workers report that their pay and conditions are determined by collective agreement, and even this figure may make unions seem less important than they actually are.[8] Less than a half of all UK employees are in a workplace where no union is active.

Where trade unions *are* recognised, they often succeed in obtaining improved conditions for their members. The hourly earnings of union members, according to the Labour Force Survey, averaged £13.60 in 2009, or around one-sixth more than the average earnings of non-members (£11.80 per hour).[9]

Since 2000, unions with the support of a majority of workers in any grade have been able to compel their employers to accept recognition. There is a complex statutory process setting out the conditions in which this right is granted,[10] overseen by a specialist Tribunal, the Central Arbitration Committee (CAC). Hearings have been sought by unions before the CAC in circumstances including (for example) where the company employed only a small workforce and there was evidence of overwhelming support (and so, it was suggested, a ballot was unnecessary),[11] as well as where only 40 per cent of workers had signed up. In the latter example, the workers were recruited in the face of the surveillance of union meetings by the employer and the publication by the employer of anti-union briefings (suggesting that 'real' support for recognition was more than 40 per cent[12]). In a third case, the issue was whether the union had majority support when 44 per cent of workers had signed petitions favouring recognition (and 16 per cent were members), but workers had voted against recognition in previous ballots.[13]

Where unions are recognised, representatives of the employer will meet periodically with representatives of the union to discuss the terms and conditions of work. Across different industries, many different forms of voluntary collective bargaining can be found. Most often, a group of managers representing a single employer will meet with a single recognised union, although in some workplaces an employer will meet with two or more recognised unions at once. In addition, collective bargaining may take place at any level: from the shop, section, or office, up to the workplace, the employer as whole, or even across an entire industry.

The purpose of collective bargaining is to secure agreement between managers and workers. Where formal bargaining takes place but there is no agreement, the result may be that the union declares a collective dispute. Ultimately, the most powerful weapon in any union's possession is the threat of strike action.

There is no general right in the UK to strike.[14] What the law provides is rather protection for the striker against being sued by her employer or by a member of the public for breach of contract, and even this protection is heavily circumscribed, as a result of anti-union laws passed by Parliament in the 1980s and early 1990s. The workers involved in industrial action are protected only if the purpose of the strike is industrial and not political, and if the union ballots its members and notifies the employer both in advance of the ballot and afterwards of its result.[15]

Although the negotiation of workplace rights is most commonly done through formal structures of trade union representation, it is also the case that increasing numbers of workers represent their fellow workers during workplace disputes (whether a union is formally recognised by the employer or not). At times, this situation results from mechanisms detailed in statute, as for example, where an employer seeks to make large numbers of workers redundant and there is no recognised union in the workplace. In these circumstances, the employer is in any event required to consult workplace representatives, who must be elected or appointed by the workers.[16] Employers also must consult with workers regarding fixed-term employees' rights,[17] health and safety at work,[18] maternity and parental leave,[19] occupational pensions,[20] transfers of an undertaking[21] and working time.[22] The duty to consult applies irrespective of whether or not there is a recognised union.

In addition, workers have the right to be accompanied by a colleague or a union official in any grievance or disciplinary procedure.[23] The exercise of this right in non-union workplaces varies enormously. There are employers who try to ignore the right altogether (and fail to mention the right, for example, in their standard letters requiring workers to attend disciplinary meetings). There are others who will allow a range of different representatives to attend, from family members to qualified lawyers. Some colleagues in a disciplinary hearing do no more than take notes on behalf of a friend. Others will 'put a case' on behalf of the threatened worker. Some will know as much law and be as confident as a trained union representative.

There are other ways in which workplace negotiations can take place even without a recognised union, as for example, where the employer recognises a works council or staff forum. In some small workplaces, the employer may in practice bargain over pay and conditions with select senior employees. In any workplace, where a particular matter becomes of great concern to large numbers of employees, letters or petitions to managers may result in de facto negotiations. Indeed, studies of even the lowest-paid and most vulnerable workers suggest that they usually try to raise their concerns with their managers, either individually or by joining with co-workers to complain, although their complaints are often ignored.[24]

There is, in short, an enormous diversity of collective workplace negotiation, taking in formal meetings, informal meetings, letters, and a myriad other processes besides. All these dynamics are, of course, more common where there is a union, but it would be wrong to assume that they are only found where a union is present, or only where the union is recognised under a written agreement with the employer.

* * *

The first chapter of this book looks at *how* and *when* workers lose Tribunal cases. By 'lose', I mean more than whether a claim is upheld by the court (for example, whether it is found that an act was an act of discrimination, or that wages were unlawfully deducted or that a dismissal was unfair). I argue that a claimant can also be said to have lost if the claimant wants her job back and she does not get it back, or if she obtains a finding of discrimination or unfair dismissal and an award is made but it is significantly less than the worker's actual loss, or if the Tribunal orders compensation but the employer never actually pays. Chapter 1 addresses the various stages at which a claimant may find that the claim turns against them to their employer's advantage. Along the way, I hope to give those without experience of the Tribunal system a sense of how a typical hearing is conducted. But this book is above all a policy intervention, rather than a 'how to' guide.

Chapter 2 begins the analysis of *why* workers lose. It explores the historical origins of the Tribunal system, which date back to the Industrial Relations Act 1971, behind which stood the Donovan Commission of 1965–68. Many of the choices of that commission still shape Tribunals, including the decisions that the way to create an employment court system was by expanding the existing Tribunals (a court in which a legally trained Judge was likely to dominate), and to take no active steps to make reinstatement (rather than compensation) the main remedy for unfair dismissal.

The next three chapters look at important groups of workers with distinct experiences of the Employment Tribunal. Chapter 3 considers agency workers, who in recent years have been increasingly deprived of the key remedy of unfair dismissal. Chapter 4 considers the reasons for the increased number of equal pay claims, whose cases are now among the most numerous of claims submitted to the Tribunal each year. Chapter 5 considers reasons for the very low rates of success of claimants in race discrimination cases.

Chapter 6 looks at the use of the European Convention of Human Rights in employment litigation, contrasting the relative absence of human rights-inspired victories in employment law to their presence in other areas of law.

Chapter 7 looks at the relationship between trade unions and what I term the 'Employment Tribunal system', by which I mean not just these courts, but their dominance of areas which 30 or 40 years ago were usually considered the domain of collective bargaining. One theme of this book is that the incursion of law into employment disputes over matters such as dismissals has weakened the position of workers themselves and of their unions in particular, who are much better placed than Tribunals to act as the guardians of workers' interests.

Chapter 8 argues that there are foundations to the UK's legal culture, which mean that the increasing 'juridification' of individual employment rights (that is, the tendency for them to be resolved by legal rather than non-legal means) will inevitably tend to result in the disappointment of those workers who rely on the law. These include the amenability of the common law towards property rights, the tradition in the common law of reading contracts (including employment contracts) literally, and the subjectivity of the key common law concept of 'reasonableness'.

Chapter 9 considers recent attempts to alter the balance between the parties in the Tribunal, including the Employment Acts of 2002 (introducing statutory dispute resolution procedures) and 2008 (repealing the same procedures) and, most recently, the proposals of the present Coalition government to increase the qualifying service required before a worker can bring an unfair dismissal claim to two years, and to introduce a hearing fee which would be paid by claimants before they could start a claim, both of which proposals are from a worker's perspective malign. These proposals are summarised as of the date of writing (1 September 2011); by the time that this book is read, it is likely that at least some of them will have come into effect.

In the Conclusion, certain alternative proposals are put for the reform of the Tribunals, including the replacement of compensation with reinstatement as the primary remedy for unfair dismissal. The book concludes with an argument in favour of the de-juridification of individual employment rights and the restoration of individual disputes to their ideal context of workplace bargaining.

1
The Tribunal Obstacle Race

Tribunals are popularly believed to be non-legalistic, non-bureaucratic, and suitable for lay people to use whereas the opposite is nearer the truth.[1]

His Honour Judge McMullen QC: Why did you submit your appeal late?
Miss Chidodo: Because I am poor and could not afford a lawyer.[2]

'Mum awarded £50k payout',[3] 'Sacked school assistant wins nearly £40,000',[4] 'Council chief who fell victim to ageism in line for £1m.'[5] If everything we read in the papers were true, it would follow that the Tribunal is a benign lottery in which workers, by no more effort than simply attending court, are awarded huge pay-outs. In part because of this reporting, as well as because of policy decisions taken by both Conservative and Labour Governments, the number of Tribunal claims has increased from around 15,000 cases per year in the early 1970s, to double that figure by the end of the 1980s, 70,000 cases per year by 1992–93, 100,000 cases in a year for the first time in the financial year 1995–96, and 218,100 claims in 2010–11.[6]

Yet set against this rosy picture of repeated Tribunal victories is the different story told by claimants, many of whom look back on litigation as among the most unpleasant experience of their working lives. Many Tribunal claimants describe feeling unhappiness as a result of litigation. Some 33 per cent of all claimants (and 43 per cent of all discrimination claimants) report suffering anxiety or depression as a result of their case.[7] Lawyers refer to this phenomenon as 'litigation stress',[8] and while some feeling of unease is perhaps inevitable for all litigants, irrespective of the court in which they appear, there is something especially wearying about Employment Tribunal claims. Here, for example, are the views of three former claimants, who were interviewed in 2006 on their experiences of bringing Tribunal claims:

> I became financially in debt because I wasn't able to meet my regular domestic bills ... I'm still trying to catch up on bills and things that got left. I'm trying to clear up this mess. The £3,000

> was like a month's wages, it went back against the bills. It wasn't luxury money. Financially, I'm still struggling.
>
> Physically and emotionally it took months to get over it and I was traumatised and weakened by it. You don't know what's going on, you're in it and all I knew is that I was having to deal with this solicitor and getting no support and becoming anxious and crying, shaking.
>
> I think it has affected me in that my tolerance for stress is less than it used to be. I am weaker.[9]

Of the above claimants, the first settled the case in advance of a hearing, and of the other two, one succeeded at a Tribunal hearing and one failed. In so far as they were paid, two out of three could be said to have 'won'. When even successful claimants look back on their case with regret, something of significance must be wrong.

The purpose of this chapter is to set out some of the ways in which Tribunal litigation goes wrong. Here, I describe *how* workers lose, later chapters ask *why*.

CHOOSING A REPRESENTATIVE

The cases which succeed at a hearing typically have the backing of a trade union (or a law centre or a Citizens Advice Bureau (CAB) or the claimant's legal fees are covered by their home contents insurance), with a solicitor representing the claimant up to the final hearing and then either a solicitor or a barrister providing advocacy at that hearing. Ideally, from the claimant's perspective, all this will be done without them having to pay for the lawyers involved. Of those who are not advised or represented by a trade union or law centre or CAB but who fund their case themselves, some claimants go directly to a high street or to a specialist employment solicitor and obtain representation by paying an hourly fee or by agreeing to be represented on a no-win no-fee basis. The effect of no-win no-fee agreements is to reduce both the risk of litigation (a losing claimant will not have to pay towards their own or the other side's costs) and its potential benefit (a typical fee is around 50 per cent of the claimant's award, if they win; while no-win no-fee contracts may contain stiff penalty clauses if, for example, the claimant disagrees with their representative and decides to appoint a new representative midway through their case).

Where the worker is not a member of a union but there is a recognised union in the workplace, the union may be willing to advise or represent the non-member at an internal hearing, such as where the worker brings a grievance against her manager but has no intention of taking the claim subsequently to a Tribunal. In those sorts of circumstances, the union would normally find a lay union representative to represent the worker (representing a non-member well at an internal grievance or disciplinary hearing is often an effective way to recruit that non-member to the union).

Things are more difficult in situations such as threatened dismissals, where it may be clear from the start that the worker will be sacked and that if she seeks redress she will have to bring a Tribunal claim. Unions often limit representation to those of its members who have been already paying subs for at least six months before the hearing. While the rule means that fewer people get assistance, it unfortunately makes necessary commercial sense for the union. Tribunal cases are expensive. It makes no sense for non-members to gain the full benefits of membership without having contributed when their job seemed more secure.

In an ordinary dismissal of a trade union member for misconduct, the responsibility for the claimant's case might be passed on as illustrated in Table 1.1.

Table 1.1 Procedure for claimant's case

Period:	*1* *Disciplinary hearing*	*2* *Dismissal hearing*	*3* *Claim form*	*4* *Case management discussion*	*5* *Tribunal hearing*
Likely representative	Lay union rep	Regional official	Regional official	Union solicitor	Barrister

There are very many variations on this pattern. The sequence would be different if the case involved a point of principle of wide importance to the union (national officials might get involved rather than regional ones, or regional officials might get involved earlier), or if the case looked likely to be settled, or if the underlying law was particularly complex (the union might instruct a barrister at an early stage), or if the prospects of success were less than 50 per cent, or indeed if the union was a small one (so that cases would have to be handled by an outside firm of solicitors).

In disputes which threaten to go as far as the Tribunal, the claimant will need the backing of one of her union's regional or national officials. Assuming an official is found to back her case, the official may refuse to get involved until the date of the Tribunal hearing is known. If officials advised every member with a simple grievance, they would be overwhelmed with work. In some cases, the official will do no more than request an initial assessment of the member's chances of success. The purpose of assessment is to decide whether to pass the case on to the union's lawyers. Five years ago, most unions would provide legal representation for a member with a 50 per cent or better chance of success. Where budgets are squeezed, it may be that even better prospects are needed before the union agrees to represent the worker.

If the claimant is supported by a local law centre or a CAB, she will be assessed to see whether civil legal aid, which is administered by the Legal Services Commission (LSC), will fund her case. In legislation which is presently before Parliament,[10] the government proposes to restrict legal aid in employment to discrimination cases only. Until that bill is passed and comes into effect, all employment tribunal cases are capable of being funded by legal aid, irrespective of jurisdiction (that is, whether they are wages, dismissal, or discrimination claims). The chief filtering mechanism is that cases may only be supported where the client's means are sufficiently modest so that she is eligible for legal aid. The rule is that the claimant and her partner between them must have a monthly disposable income (the difference between salary and rent or mortgage) of no more than £733 (in 2011–12).[11] Even before the present Coalition government had been elected, attempts were being made to reduce legal aid spending, by freezing the eligibility rate and not increasing it with rising prices. A 2008 estimate based on data from the Family Resources Survey, an annual survey of 28,000 UK households, suggested that only 29 per cent of the population of England and Wales was eligible for civil legal aid; a proportion dramatically less than just five years before.[12] Even where a client is eligible, the solicitor is ordinarily paid a fixed fee of just £302 (in October 2010)[13] by the Legal Service Commission (LSC), for each of meeting clients, sending a letter of advice, drafting claim forms, reading and responding to any pre-trial correspondence, producing bundles, seeking disclosure of documents from the respondent, drafting the claimant's witness statement, interviewing other witnesses and settling the case. Crucially, representation at the Tribunal hearing is *not* funded by legal aid; the LSC's assumption is that a claimant will get a fair hearing if they attend without a representative[14] and have to put their case directly to the Tribunal.[15]

Even where a claimant obtains representation, by either of these routes, she still faces obstacles. To maximise her chances, the claimant needs not just any old representative but someone with the skills to advance her case. A good trade union representative is someone of real value. The representative may know the company's procedures by heart and be able to spot even relatively minor breaches by the employer. The representative may have lengthy experience of working with a particular manager and have developed the skills to persuade that manager to change his or her mind before a final decision is made. She may have a good understanding of what she needs to do to keep the claimant's case alive. She may be well connected to the union's legal networks, so that the claimant's case is taken up seamlessly by an official and then the solicitor or barrister who will represent the claimant at an eventual Tribunal hearing. Best of all, she will have access to sources of strength that are wholly closed to the lawyer. For example, there may a group of colleagues who can rally behind the claimant, who could come forward as witnesses to a hearing, or who may even threaten strike action if the company does not back down. But the trade union movement is a movement of volunteers. Some union representatives have had little training in employment law, others have sought training but have been refused time off by their employer,[16] and in any event only a minority of those who have been trained are familiar with the most recent changes to the law. A trade unionist's skills are in workplace negotiation. If the average representative had the same legal skills as an ordinary lawyer, they would be a lawyer and not a trade unionist; they would presumably be better paid.

Even at the earliest stages, before Tribunal proceedings are contemplated, it is possible for an enthusiastic but under-trained representative to damage a claimant's case, for example, by encouraging a claimant not to make serious allegations against a fellow worker which might antagonise the manager hearing the case. Caution is sensible in internal workplace disputes; it can be destructive later. If the claimant fails to raise a matter early on, and a complaint is raised for the first time in a Tribunal claim form, that part of the claim risks being struck out, or an award can be reduced for the claimant's failure to follow the correct procedure, or the Tribunal may simply disbelieve the complaint: 'If you thought you were being harassed', the question will be asked, 'why didn't you complain of harassment at the time?'

Finally, the claimant's difficulties are not less but just different if, rather than having union representation, she makes an initial approach to a solicitor in private practice. Cost and time pressures ensure that the client will spend much time with trainees rather than experienced caseworkers. High street solicitors will see a case differently from a union representative, they are, for example, more likely to take internal hearings for granted (as they will usually not be allowed to attend them).

The primary disadvantage of going to a private solicitor is of course that the claimant will have to pay their fees: solicitor rates' can be of the order of £150–300 an hour,[17] while few barristers would agree to appear at a Tribunal for less than £500–800 per day, and some barristers (typically, a certain class of respondent's representative), will charge their clients fees of up to £1000 per hour.

COMPLETING THE CLAIM FORM

A second key moment comes with the claimant's decision to submit a claim to the Tribunal. This is done by completing a ('ET1') claim form, which can be found online.[18] Most of the information is relatively straightforward: name, address, salary, date of dismissal (if dismissed). The most difficult question on the form is the one where the claimant is given an opportunity to set out the essential details of her case.

The accuracy expected by the Tribunal of the information given in this section of the form will depend on whether the claimant is represented by a lawyer or not. A claimant who has legal representation will be expected to complete this form with precision; but where the claimant does not have representation the Tribunal should normally take a more permissive attitude. Usually, an unrepresented litigant will have the opportunity to cure any defects in their claim form at a subsequent Case Management Discussion (CMD). At such a hearing, the Tribunal may, for example, invite an unrepresented claimant to provide further and better particulars of her case. Assuming the claimant does so, this procedure will cause her no prejudice.

The Tribunal's reaction to the information in the form represents a compromise between two directly opposed ways of thinking. One approach is to treat the information in the form as legal 'pleadings', that is, the client's formal case, and equivalent, say, to the documents produced by large corporations when they litigate in high-profile proceedings, such as claims before the High Court. There is a very deep-rooted notion in English law that pleadings should be read carefully, critically, and if need be strictly against the party relying on them. Now this tradition makes greater sense when speaking of a corporation, whose commercial documents will be written by professionals with time to spare. If a company has set out their case in a shoddy fashion so that a possible defence is missed, it should not be able to benefit from its own incompetence. Equally, it would make little sense to expect the same standards of an unrepresented claimant, who may have undergone any level of formal education, and who will not be familiar with the terms lawyers use. If, say, a claimant used the word 'discrimination' when strictly they meant 'harassment' (or vice versa), it would be unfair to punish her for an innocent mistake.

That said, there is great pressure on Tribunal time. Employment Judges prefer cases to be as short and as focused as possible, with the most time available for them to concentrate on the fewest possible issues, so that they can give their decision the care and attention that it deserves. If at a CMD a Judge can persuade a claimant to withdraw as many parts of the case as the claimant is willing to do, especially those parts of it which are poorly pleaded, the Judge at the CMD will have done a considerable service to the Judge in charge of the final hearing.

If these were the strongest parts of the case, and the Judge was wrong when persuading the claimant to drop them, they may have done the claimant a disservice, as the claimant will not (save exceptionally) be allowed to revive them later.

PREPARING FOR THE HEARING

Even where the claimant has found a lawyer, and their claim has been put in a proper fashion, difficulties remain. Lawyers set themselves goals which are not the claimant's. They speak to each other in an obscure language, which mystifies the lay person as much as it directs attention to the real issues. Take, for example, the word 'victimisation'; to most non-lawyers, this means being made a victim for an unfair reason, as in 'I was victimised because of my race.' The law, by contrast, defines victimisation as something more specific, as when a worker is punished because she has made, or has supported a colleague's, previous complaint: 'the employer victimised Janet, because she had been a witness at John's grievance hearing.'

The pre-hearing steps are over-complex, as lawyers flaunt their knowledge of Tribunal procedure. Aggressive respondent solicitors will send letters to claimants in language suggesting that their requests are in fact orders: 'The claimant is compelled … .' To make matters worse, they may print the documents in the same font as the case management decision of the Tribunals themselves, causing the unwary unrepresented litigant to believe these are bona fide orders of the Tribunal.

It can take a very long time to bring an employment claim to a resolution. Even a standard unfair dismissal case will usually be heard six to nine months after the claimant submits their claim form. Where preliminary hearings are appealed by either side, the full merits hearing may take place as much as two years after the claim was submitted. Where a full merits decision is appealed, the process can drag on for years. Where a claimant leaves their employment in poor mental or physical health and with a strong sense of injustice about their treatment, the delays add to their stress and can prevent the claimant from fully recovering.

In 2010–11, some 61 per cent of cases were settled or withdrawn, that is, disposed outside a hearing.[19] In theory, the propensity to settle benefits both the claimant and the respondent. On both sides, costs are reduced if a claim can be settled without a hearing. In settlement, claimants receive something, and in that sense this outcome is a 'victory' for them. Seen from the employer's perspective, the rationale for settlement is even greater. Because Tribunals are usually a 'no costs' jurisdiction and even an unsuccessful party will not pay the other side's costs, save in exceptional cases, the employer has an extremely strong incentive to settle. One risk of the hearing for the employer is that it may succeed, but only after having incurred a bill of several thousand pounds in legal costs, to which the claimant will not ordinarily be required to contribute anything. It is sensible therefore for the respondent to propose settlement at a figure of (say) half their likely costs. If the offer is accepted, the employer will emerge from the process out of pocket, but much less so than they would have done if they had fought the case to a hearing and *won*.

So far, the dynamic of settlement would seem to benefit the claimant. But settlement brings problems for the claimant too. The consciousness of the likelihood of settlement distorts the litigation strategy of some claimant representatives. It encourages some representatives to 'aim high', to put a value on a case out of all proportion to what is likely to be achieved at the hearing. This tactic is designed to boost the settlement point. It also gives the claimant a false idea of the value of their claim. As the hearing comes nearer, the worst representative switches round. Having previously over-sold the claimant's case now they under-value it. Where the claimant is represented by a 'no win no fee' lawyer, settlement means for the representative a guarantee of payment; while continuing with the case to a hearing means that all outcomes are possible, including the claimant's defeat (and the lawyer going unpaid). In the final stages of settlement, the claimant's representative may encourage the claimant to accept a settlement offer from the employer which is significantly less than the value which the same representative had given the client in advising her on the merits of her case. Thus, even a settlement that is higher than what she would have won at a hearing can feel like a defeat for the claimant.

One unacknowledged scandal of settlement proceedings is the pressure put on respondents by their own solicitors' fees, some of which are astronomical. Companies overpay for legal advice because of ignorance (they do not shop around for legal advice) and because senior managers put a high premium on the protection of their own reputations. Consider the example of a claimant who is represented on legal aid, whose solicitor is paid around £300 for the whole case, and whose barrister (if she has one) will almost certainly be representing the client pro bono (that is, for free). While the going rate for respondents' representatives is around £150–300 per hour, it is not unheard of for respondent lawyers to charge £1,000 per hour. Every experienced claimant representative will have been in many cases where the other side was billing ten to fifteen times as much for the case as they were.

Moreover, experience teaches that the same employer representatives who over-bill their own side are also most aggressive in litigation, especially towards unrepresented claimants. Many perfectly good claims are withdrawn by claimants in response to letters from respondent solicitors, often long before the hearing, informing unemployed or low-paid workers that their cases are hopeless (whether they are or not) and threatening the claimant with the employer's costs of tens of thousands of pounds, representing for the company a few seconds of trading and for the worker their entire life's savings. The injustice of the withdrawal of good claims under costs pressure, which was relatively unusual five or ten years ago, has become pervasive in recent years. Indeed, the present government proposes to facilitate costs applications by employers, a policy which could have no possible consequence other than to encourage precisely this sort of costs blackmail.

THE HEARING ITSELF

The Employment Tribunal is often characterised as an industrial jury;[20] the idea being that the there are three members on the panel, of different but equal status. In practice, Tribunals are dominated by the Employment Judge (known until December 2007 as the Tribunal 'chair').[21] The Judge is a lawyer. The other two 'wing' members are chosen for their expertise of industrial relations, one from the management side and the other from an employee perspective. The Judge will ask the majority of the questions. Afterwards, the Judge will write the first draft of the judgment. One 1985 study took the unusual step of interviewing lay panellists on their experiences. Three members expressed their frustration that, in practice, the Judge dominates:

> (1) Case law and legal decisions can sometimes upset what may be as plain as a pikestaff.
> (2) If a case depends on legal rulings the lay member has no choice, one must remember that 'the law' is not always 'justice'.
> (3) Irrespective of the submissions of the parties, the 'legal reality' must take precedence.[22]

The panel members sometimes outvote the Judge. One case, from 2007, concerned an alcoholic employee who was dismissed for being drunk at work. The employer's alcohol policy provided for suspension of disciplinary procedures where an employee sought assistance to cure his alcoholism. The employer failed to provide a copy of the alcohol policy to the employee until immediately before the hearing which took the decision to dismiss. The ET found by a 2–1 majority that the employee had been unfairly dismissed, with the two panel members outvoting the Judge.[23] Another case from 2007 involved a trade unionist who had given a newspaper interview about conditions in his plant and was dismissed afterwards. The company said that the worker had been fairly dismissed for reasons of making untrue allegations. The worker said that he had been unfairly dismissed for trade union activities. The Employment Tribunal found by a 2–1 majority that the claimant had been unfairly dismissed.[24] Both decisions were later reversed on appeal.[25]

The British legal system acknowledges that some courts are more accessible than others. For example, a child accused of robbery will have her case heard in a Youth Court. In contrast to an adult facing the same charge, she will be addressed throughout the hearing by her first name only. In court, there will be a number of adults, any of whom can address the court in her support, including her parents, social workers and probation officers. The language of the hearing is relaxed and relatively informal. The Youth Court is a much more accessible court than the adult Magistrates' Court, on which it is based and in which it is normally housed.

Applying the same logic, Tribunals are supposed to be accessible courts. The 1968 Report of the Donovan Commission, from which the modern Tribunal system dates, announced that the Tribunals would be 'easily accessible, informal, speedy and inexpensive'.[26] Tribunals, in the words of another 1973 account:

> ... are cheap; they are geographically convenient to use; they are open to all litigants, in person or represented as they wish; and their procedures are specifically designed to be used, with help readily available if he requires it, by the man in the street.[27]

Yet many litigants find Tribunals closed and off-putting places. The language of the court is highly formal. The procedure of Tribunals is fixed. Parties address the court in a fixed order. Factual submissions are made before legal submissions. To be most effective in putting their case, even an unrepresented claimant will be expected to copy some of the mannerisms of an experienced barrister addressing a higher court.

Another part of the complexity of the Tribunals is the tendency for the number of documents involved in every claim to grow, case by case, and year by year. One Tribunal case from 2007 concerned a senior partner at a UK law firm. The firm reorganised its pension scheme, with the result that those who retired at 55 would receive a significantly more generous pension than those who retired at 54. In the aftermath of the adoption of the scheme, the partner retired. He was 54 years old. In its judgment, the Tribunal referred in passing to the quantity of documents that had been before it:

> Both parties put in opening skeleton arguments and the respondent, shortly after the evidence commenced, also submitted a note as to the effect of schedule 5 of the Regulations. The Tribunal was provided with 17 bundles of documents, 12 chronological bundles, a bundle containing the various versions of the Memorandum of Terms of Partnership, two bundles of inter-parties' correspondence, a bundle of witness statements, and a pleadings bundle comprising the pleadings, questionnaires, case management orders and the agreed documents referred to separately.[28]

From a reading of the judgment, it would appear that no more than 1 per cent of the material actually before the Tribunal had any effect on its decision.

Many claimants complain after their case that they did not receive a fair hearing from the Tribunal system. In 1989, the Equal Opportunities Commission published a study of the views of claimants in sex discrimination claims. A number of the interviewees clearly felt very badly let down by the final hearing:

> (1) The chairman ... completely dominated both the others on the bench. He twisted and turned things to the company's advantage.
> (2) I had a feeling that the members of the bench were on the employer's side.
> (3) I was led by all sources to believe that a Tribunal was conducted with informality and was more or less an open discussion. This isn't so. We did not sit round the table. The witness is in a box,[29] takes an oath and has questions fired at them with such a speed the brain numbs. The chairman who fired the questions at me did so like a machine gun.
> (4) I thought that the chairman's behaviour was disgracefully biased right from the start.
> (5) My experience was that I was fighting both the defendants and the Tribunal.[30]

Tribunals are environments in which respondents very often (but certainly not always) get a more sympathetic hearing than claimants. There are many reasons for this. Witnesses for each side are expected to answer questions. Establishing that a witness is lying is a matter of linguistic power. If a witness does not answer a question precisely, they will find that the Employment Judge will back up the barrister or the solicitor who is doing the questioning. It will feel as if there are two lawyers cross-examining them at once. People who have spent more years in formal education almost inevitably find the process more congenial than those without. Those with English as a first language are more likely to prosper, those without are less likely to succeed. Managers are usually better educated and often more familiar with Tribunal procedure and come over to the Tribunal as better witnesses.

Employers tend to spend more money defending their cases; they hire a better class of representative: a QC rather than a junior barrister, a barrister rather than a solicitor, a specialist employment solicitor rather than a high street solicitor, a solicitor rather than a union official. Although it does occasionally happen, employers are much less likely to run the risk of appearing at the Tribunal without a legal representative of one sort or another. Another 2006 survey invited applicants in race cases to describe their experiences of the Tribunal. One theme was the surprise of claimants at the resource the company would devote to fighting their case:

> (1) What I didn't know was the formality of it. I thought it was three people behind a desk. You sit on one side, the prisoner[31] sits on the other, you put your case forward, and someone comes to a decision. I thought I was going to be up against my managers. I didn't expect barristers.
> (2) I was being assisted by a friend, and the employer is in a better or bigger position or may [have] more legal knowledge, I never thought they would be using a solicitor.
> (3) When we had the directions hearing they hired a QC. They have four to five partners who concentrate on employment law, plus staff.[32]

Employers also come over better at Tribunals because they are usually better briefed. In all likelihood, they will have more experience of previous Tribunal litigation, they have a clearer idea of what to expect, and also because they hold a greater supply of one commodity which is of real interest to a Tribunal – information. Where, for example, a claimant has been dismissed for reason of incapability, the Tribunal will want to know what sort of procedure was followed. Any sensible questioning inevitably goes to the content of discussions at meetings at which the claimant was probably absent. Did the claimant's manager have a discussion with the head of training? Was there any consideration of what the company could do to give the employee a second chance? Was the case discussed with other managers; and what was said? When was the decision to dismiss really made? A Tribunal can ask a claimant for this information but usually she will not have it. Her line manager, who was present at those meetings, is naturally a better source for the Tribunal.

A number of legal doctrines have the effect of tilting legal proceedings in favour of employers. For example, the determination of whether a dismissal was fair or unfair is governed by section 98(4) of the Employment Rights Act 1996:

> (4) … the determination of the question whether the dismissal is fair or unfair (having regard to the reason shown by the employer) –
>
> (a) depends on whether in the circumstances (including the size and administrative resources of the employer's undertaking) the employer acted reasonably or unreasonably in treating it as a sufficient reason for dismissing the employee, and
> (b) shall be determined in accordance with equity and the substantial merits of the case.

In determining that a dismissal is fair if the employer acted reasonably, Parliament intended that the standard of fairness would be an objective one.

Yet the employment courts have followed a different approach. As a matter of case law, when determining the fairness of a dismissal, the Tribunal is required to approach the question via the test set out in *Iceland Frozen Food* v *Jones*:[33]

> Was it reasonable for the employer to dismiss? If no reasonable employer would have dismissed him then the dismissal was unfair, but if a reasonable employer might reasonably have dismissed him, then the dismissal was fair. It must be remembered that in all these cases there is a band of reasonableness within which one employer might reasonably take one and another quite reasonably take a different view.[34]

A dismissal is not unfair if unreasonable; it is only unfair if it was *so unreasonable* that *no reasonable employer* would have dismissed. Contrary to the plain words of the act, this is not an objective standard, but a subjective test, with only a minimum residual objectivity standard.[35] In practice, the range-of-reasonable-responses test limits the role of the Tribunal to a review function. The Tribunal must not ask itself what happened. It must limit itself to asking whether the employer's decision was so bad as to be unfair. The test is equivalent to a presumption that a dismissal was fair.

Employment law exists in order to protect workers from what would otherwise be the limited safeguards provided by employment contracts, these contracts being drafted by the employer and not the worker. Yet, as I argue in later chapters, the common law is a tradition which enables the judiciary to alter the regulatory content of any statute by active interpretation – and this power has most often been exercised to limit workers' protection and safeguard managerial authority. The judicial invention of the range-of-reasonable-responses test is a good example of this process at work. Other examples of rulings which disadvantage claimants (including the policy that agency workers are not employees, as well as the judicial caution in applying the reversed burden of proof in discrimination cases) are discussed in later chapters.

Very broadly, claimants win in half of all unfair dismissal claims, while in discrimination claims a clear majority of claimants lose.[36] But the dynamics which cause a majority of employers to settle have the odd consequence that the largest number of claims to go to a hearing are ones where the dispute between the employer and the claimant is relatively superficial (such as claims for non-payment of wages). While these are only a small proportion of the claims submitted to the Tribunal, they are a very large proportion of the cases which come before a Judge. Indeed, it is rare that a worker who brings a wages or breach of contract claim will leave the Tribunal with no remedy at all. In these sorts of cases, both claimants and respondents are often unrepresented. The hearings themselves may last as little as an hour or even less. Maybe the employer simply miscalculated the amount of wages owed to the claimant. In the large majority of cases, the worker will not have gone to the trouble of forcing a hearing unless at least some money was owed to her.

Looking at the system as a whole, a clear majority (currently three-fifths) of Tribunal cases that go to a full merits hearing are won by claimants.[37] But against this figure it has to be observed that the longer and more significant a case the less a claimant's chance of success: so wages claims usually win, unfair dismissal cases can go either way, and most discrimination claims lose. So, while most claimants win at the Tribunal, most Judges spend more of their time deciding cases against claimants, and most representatives have the same experience. If a case is serious enough for the claimant to need representation, the chances are that she will lose.

REMEDY

Even success at a 'merits' hearing can be but a prelude to further disappointment. To properly win a case, the claimant needs not just an order that an unlawful deduction was made or a dismissal was unfair, she also need to succeed at a second 'remedy' (that is, compensation) stage. From a claimant's perspective, the decision of the Tribunal is almost never what was hoped. In a typical unfair dismissal case, a claimant may have three different definitions of 'victory'. First, she may desire the satisfaction of hearing from an employer or from the tribunal that she should never have been dismissed in the first place. Secondly, she may seek re-employment with the same business. Third, she may seek compensation for her economic losses since her dismissal: if she is now unemployed, or if she is now employed in worse-paid job, the difference between the money that she would have earned if she had not been sacked and what she has in fact received.

A 2006 survey of 40 claimants in race discrimination cases, found that a large number of claimants prioritised the first of these possible outcomes:

> (1) [The Tribunal chair] said 'You haven't put any damages or claim'. I said, 'I'm not interested in money. I want justice.'
> (2) I expected [the company] to simply say sorry. I was not expecting a lot of money. I wanted a Tribunal to tell them they had done wrong … .
> (3) I wanted them reprimanded and opened to the scrutiny of people outside the organisation so other people could see what they were doing.
> (4) The main issue was that I was abused and all my people were abused and nothing was going to be done about that and they just wanted to bury the hatchet. Them apologising and bringing the man to book is much better than offering me money.
> (5) I wanted to speak for the downtrodden, those people who are being discriminated against. It wasn't any remuneration per se. I wanted those cowboy employers [to] be brought to book.[38]

Yet the reward even for a successful claim is financial compensation for the claimant rather than a public declaration of the employer's fault.[39]

Moreover, while the Employment Tribunal does have the power to order the reinstatement or re-engagement of a dismissed claimant, this power is hardly ever used in practice. Of the 40,000 plus unfair dismissal claims before the Tribunal in 2010–11, only *eight* cases concluded with orders from the Tribunal reinstating or re-engaging the claimant.[40] In the early years of the Tribunal system, these orders were more common, but even then they were rare (see Table 1.2).

Tribunals have the power to order reinstatement or re-engagement, yet where a claimant is awarded these remedies, and the employer declines to act on the Tribunal's order, there is no sanction other than an increased financial penalty.

Table 1.2 Reinstatement or re-engagement orders in all dismissal cases (select years)[41]

1972	*1974*	*1976*	*1978*	*1980*
4.4%	4.3%	5.5%	3.2%	2.8%

The failure to reinstate is one of the worst problems of the Tribunal system. Employers know that Tribunals will not reinstate successful claimants; and, armed by that knowledge, they do not reinstate employees where an employee is dismissed and the employee appeals the dismissal. Experienced employment advisers treat reinstatement at an internal appeal as an extraordinary outcome: to be celebrated as such when it happens, and ignored without regret when it does not.[42]

The position of a claimant who is reinstated is preferable to the position of a claimant who is compensated but not reinstated in the following ways. First, the reinstated claimant has her old job back. It is the routine experience of representing claimants that they will tell you that their job was perfectly suited to them, and they had many friends at work, except that a new manager wanted to make his name by volunteering for cuts to his department, or a junior manager felt insecure and determined to remove the claimant, or a colleague decided to bully her. None of these scenarios would prevent reinstatement, but for the pervasive approach of employers which is to protect either the managers who made the original decision or the managers who decided not to properly investigate the worker's grievance.

Secondly, the reinstated claimant has a job. Imagine the situation of, for example, a skilled construction worker dismissed by his employer for misconduct in the summer of 2008 whose case came to a hearing in the autumn of 2009. Before dismissal, the worker would have expected to remain in secure employment for the indefinite future. After dismissal, the construction industry having gone into crisis, the worker's prospects of finding similar work would be dramatically reduced. Even if she succeeded with her claim, and was compensated for losses to the date of the hearing, her chances of finding a similar well-paid job thereafter might be very remote. A rare Tribunal might compensate the worker generously for her likely future losses. But having lost a plum job, the claimant faces potentially years of underemployment. Tribunals are cautious about making awards to compensate workers for future losses, not least because it is difficult for the employer to revisit these cases when a worker goes on to find work more quickly than expected.

Third, even where a claimant both receives compensation and finds a suitable new job at the same salary, she is still worse off than a reinstated worker. The latter returns to a workplace in which she has already worked in all likelihood for at least a year (if the worker did not have a year's continuous service she would not be able to bring a claim). She returns to colleagues whom she knows, and to a work environment in which she should retain the credit for her good employment prior to dismissal. The reinstated worker also has the protection of the rights to claim unfair dismissal; her newly appointed counterpart must wait for a year (from April 2012 two years) before she has the same rights.

For all these reasons, reinstatement is the obvious and best solution to a typical unfair dismissal; the basic unavailability of reinstatement (or even re-engagement) reduces the rights of workers as a group.

The problems of compensation can also be seen by looking at the amounts of compensation available in the ordinary Tribunal case. The median award made by way of compensation for unfair dismissal was just £4,591 in 2010–11,[43] or roughly double the amount that the average claimant spends on legal fees (£2,493).[44] At Tribunal, only around half of claims succeed. This suggests that the half of all Tribunal claimants who win will have achieved a net gain of around £2,000, while many of the other half who have lost will have to pay their own legal fees equivalent to around 10 per cent of the average wage.[45] 'Even if you win, and that is not easy', one critic of the Tribunals has written, 'you generally end up with peanuts.'[46]

Tribunal awards are made low by the operation of hostile statutory rules and the unwillingness of Employment Judges to make awards outside a narrow band that the Judges consider reasonable. As an example of the former process; the compensation for unfair dismissal combines two elements: a basic award calculated in a fixed statutory ratio, and a compensatory award which is intended to reflect the financial loss a claimant has suffered as a result of dismissal. Under the basic award, claimants are compensated for dismissal at the rate of one week's salary for every year that the claimant has been continuously employed. For no good reason at all, when calculating a claimant's compensation under the basic award, the remedy is limited to £400 per week,[47] or less than four-fifths of the average salary.

Moreover, claimants tend to lose out under the compensatory scheme because Tribunals start from the actual losses of a claimant and then subject this figure to one or more potential down-lifts. The relevant statute is section 123 of the Employment Rights Act, the relevant subsections of which provide that

> (1) ... the amount of the compensatory award shall be such amount as the tribunal considers just and equitable in all the circumstances having regard to the loss sustained by the complainant in consequence of the dismissal in so far as that loss is attributable to action taken by the employer ...
> (4) In ascertaining the loss referred to in subsection (1) the tribunal shall apply the same rule concerning the duty of a person to mitigate his loss as applies to damages recoverable under the common law of England and Wales or (as the case may be) Scotland ...
> (6) Where the tribunal finds that the dismissal was to any extent caused or contributed to by any action of the complainant, it shall reduce the amount of the compensatory award by such proportion as it considers just and equitable having regard to that finding ... .

In the ordinary run of Tribunal litigation, the section is interpreted as meaning that

- The Tribunal can reduce the remedy paid to a worker where the worker has contributed to her own dismissal; *and*
- The Tribunal can reduce the remedy paid because it would be just and equitable to do so;[48] *and*
- The Tribunal can reduce the remedy where a worker has failed to remedy her loss (for example, by not taking sufficient steps after dismissal to find a new job); *and*
- The Tribunal can reduce the remedy in circumstances where an employer could have fairly dismissed a worker, but the dismissal was unfair because a fair procedure was not followed. In these circumstances, compensation is often limited to the time it would have taken an employer to follow a fair procedure.[49]

The cumulative injustice which results when more than one of these reductions is made can be seen by considering the case of a full-time worker who was dismissed by her employer in 2008 and brought a claim against the company of unfair dismissal and race and sex discrimination. The worker won her case, but her award was subject to various reductions, which she unsuccessfully appealed in 2010. The way in which the Tribunal decided the case in her favour was by finding that she contributed to her dismissal and that her employer could fairly have dismissed her, but the dismissal was unfair in that the procedure used to dismiss her had not been a fair one. The Tribunal quantified the worker's contribution to her dismissal at 50 per cent, and limited her compensation to the length of time (a few days) it would have taken the employer to dismiss her fairly. Her eventual compensation was just £291.47.[50]

AFTER THE HEARING

Appeals are made from the Employment Tribunal to the Employment Appeal Tribunal (EAT). An unsuccessful party has no general right to appeal a case to the EAT. Most commonly, where a party applies to bring an appeal, there is a preliminary hearing to decide whether permission should be granted. In 2010–11, 218,100 claims were submitted to the Tribunal, the Tribunal held 49,300 full merits hearings, and 2,000 appeals were submitted to the EAT.[51] Where an EAT overturns all or a part of the judgment, it will normally remit the case to the same Tribunal or perhaps to a new Tribunal (depending on the extent of its criticisms of the original judgment).[52] Exceptionally, the EAT may simply decide an issue itself. From the EAT, cases can potentially, if permission is granted, be appealed to the Court of Appeal and from there to the Supreme Court. The more that different courts are involved, the greater the delay between the claim and the final decision. Where cases end at the Court of Appeal, it is not unusual for the total time between the act about which the worker complains and the final decision to be the best part of a decade.

Even for those claimants who succeed at the full merits hearing, whose award is in some sensible proportion to their actual loss, and who pick their way as required through the appeal system, this is frequently not the end of the process. Many employers simply refuse to pay the sum ordered by the Tribunal; either refusing to answer any further correspondence, or making the company insolvent to avoid the obligation to pay the debt. A study published by the Citizens Advice Bureau in 2004 gave several examples of employers simply declining to pay awards:

> A woman who sought advice from a CAB in Tyne & Wear in January 2004 had been awarded over £2,200 by an Employment Tribunal for unfair dismissal some six months previously, but had not yet received any of the award from her former employer ...
>
> A CAB in Cleveland reports assisting a man to make and pursue a Tribunal claim for unfair dismissal and unpaid wages. The claim was successful, and in January 2003, the Tribunal made an award of over £23,000. The client has never received any of the award from his former employer.
>
> A man who sought advice from a CAB in Cheshire in March 2004, had won a Tribunal award of some £40,000, but his employer was refusing to pay.[53]

A Ministry of Justice study, published in 2009, found that 18 months after their hearing, a staggering 39 per cent of successful claimants had been paid nothing by their employer whatsoever, while a further 18 per cent had been only paid part of the judgment amount.[54] Regulations have since then been made giving county court enforcement officers the responsibility for recovering Tribunal awards.[55] County courts already have a very well-established network of enforcement officers (that is, bailiffs). But the new enforcement mechanisms still require the claimant to take further steps of their own. Few employment solicitors have recent experience of the county courts, with the result that even represented claimants can suffer delays. This is yet another small measure making the Tribunals unlike what they were supposed to be – that is, industrial courts, effective, easy, and accessible to all.

For all the above reasons, employers are more enthusiastic about the experience of Tribunals than employees; in 1985, a survey of unrepresented employers and employees found that 79 percent of the former believed that their case had got across well to the Tribunal; in contrast to just 47 percent of the latter.[56]

Poor representation, case management decisions based on a legalistic reading of claim forms, a tendency to disbelieve the vulnerable, hostile legal principles enshrined in cases of some antiquity, and inadequate remedies; many of these problems can be found in isolation across different areas of the law. Their combination makes Tribunals a particularly dispiriting forum for claimants.

2
How the Tribunal System was Established

There are many who know not how to defend their causes in judgment, and there are many who do, and therefore pleaders are necessary, so that that which the plaintiffs or actors cannot, or know how not to do by themselves, they may do by their serjeants, attornies or friends.[1]

You nobody from Hell, you whore-span, you cluster of evil, you lawyer.[2]

The causes of some of the problems identified in the first chapter are no doubt legion. It would be wrong to put all the blame on politicians or Judges. One reason why successful employees in unfair dismissal cases are not reinstated is because of the weight of four decades of law-making in which the remedy has only rarely been sought, and even the most credible application has invariably been rejected. This creates a cycle of self-reinforcing behaviour, in which claimants do not ask for the remedy, their representatives fail to remind them that it is available and Judges are not asked to make reinstatement decisions. When a claimant does seek the remedy, their request inevitably is made to appear unusual and awkward.

The purpose of this chapter is to explore the history of the Tribunals since they were set up in 1964. The chapter gives one further explanation of why so many employees leave the Tribunal dissatisfied: a source of some of the various characteristic features of the present-day system, described in the last chapter, can be found in the policy decisions from which the Tribunal system was born.

What employment law was there before the Tribunals were established? A good short guide to the pre-1964 law is provided by Bill Wedderburn's *The Worker and The Law*. In a book of some 368 pages, questions of a worker's rights to sue for breach of a contract are discussed in just two sections, the first is 25 pages dealing with dismissal, and the second is 43 pages dealing with compensation for industrial accidents. By contrast, as many as 125 pages of the book deal with trade union law, addressing issues such as the legality of strikes and the rights of employers, customers, and even union members to sue unions. At various points, *The Worker and The Law* sets out a number of principles which anticipate contemporary law:

- An employer may dismiss a servant summarily for a fundamental breach of the employment contract, such as conduct amounting to a danger, or immorality, or inebriation.
- An employer may dismiss a servant summarily for repeated carelessness.
- It is for a workman to explain an absence from work.
- The employer may choose to waive the right to terminate the contract, and if he does so he cannot withdraw his waiver.
- Where a worker is wrongly dismissed, his remedy by way of damages will be the pay he would have received in his notice period.
- The purpose of damages is to compensate the worker, not punish the master.[3]

Strikingly, Wedderburn portrays written employment contracts as having greater practical significance to workers than statutory or common law rights.[4] For example, he describes a tendency for written employment contracts to grant an employer a wide discretion to dismiss. The British Overseas Airways Corporation

> ... under one agreement in 1949 acquired the right to dismiss summarily an employee for wilful neglect of their interests, for drinking intoxicating liquor or taking drugs to excess, and for disobedience or any conduct 'likely to be prejudicial to the interests of the employers'.[5]

It follows that the right to dismiss, if trammelled at all, was limited by locally negotiated obstacles. An airline pilot, accused, say, of drinking excess alcohol outside work, might appeal to a workplace committee. If the committee upheld the decision to dismiss, then the pilot might have a further right of appeal, perhaps to a more senior committee. In practice, the pilot would also in all likelihood have an effective, if unspoken, right of appeal to his fellow workers. If the pilot could persuade other workers that the sanction imposed by management was excessive, and if they took industrial action, then the threat of dismissal might be lifted. Because dismissals were likely to cause strikes, employers were dismissed infrequently compared to today.

Another account published in 1967 offered this account of disciplinary procedures in the car industry:

> Continued incompetence or breaches of Regulations may land a worker in the office. He reports to the departmental manager, who warns him in the presence of the foreman and his own shop steward, while the warning is recorded. These records are essential evidence where the final sanction of dismissal may be resorted to, or where a case may be appealed to the Personnel Office.[6]

Where a manager wished to dismiss, in short, it was by no means inevitable that dismissal would take place. A further survey from 1969 found that between 1963 and 1966, the dock labour boards dismissed on average 765 workers a year, and on average 214 were reinstated; in the building industry, meanwhile, 15 of 69 dismissal cases which were appealed to regional appeals committees between 1964 and 1967 resulted in reinstatement, and 3 of 12 dealt with at a national level had a similarly positive outcome for the worker.[7] In all these industries, internal appeal committees tended to reinstate the worker in between one-third and one-fifth of all cases.

The existence of such machinery had the practical consequence that most employment disputes took place outside the reach of the law. Thus in the 1968 edition of the contract lawyers' bible *Chitty on Contracts*, the relationship between individual and collective disputes is described in the following terms:

> In modern conditions many employees are covered by collective agreements between one or more trade unions on the one side, and one or more employers' associations on the other. In many industries, the parties on both sides have created permanent joint negotiating bodies to settle terms and conditions of employment. Much of the procedure of this collective bargaining is governed by practice, not strict law.[8]

A large employer would have a number of committees tasked with investigating disciplinary matters. In the coal industry, there were no fewer than six levels of disciplinary committee, capable of hearing appeals in an ascending vertical structure. This was an extreme example, of course. 'Many other firms', Wedderburn remarked, 'do not consult unions on disciplinary or even redundancy matters.'[9]

Already in *The Worker and The Law*, there was some discussion of the idea that specialist employment courts were needed to protect a worker's rights in employment, including in particular the worker's right not be dismissed capriciously. Wedderburn contrasted the lack of protection of trade unionists in Britain to the situation in France, where the dismissal of a workplace representative or even a former representative required the express approval of a Workers' Council or a Labour Inspector. In the UK, in a context of growing unemployment, an increasing number of unions were signing collective agreements which exchanged a promise not to strike for a guarantee of protected employment. In 1963, as Wedderburn noted, the International Labour Organization had published its Recommendation 119, in which it was suggested that dismissal should require a 'valid reason', that dismissals on discriminatory grounds should be unlawful, and that workers should have protection against dismissal.[10] 'To fulfil these recommendations', Wedderburn wrote, 'we should need either a new statute or a completely new development in our collective bargaining arrangements.'[11] That was, if anything, an understatement.

* * *

Why then were Tribunals adopted? The idea of a labour court is an old one. The first French labour courts were the *Conseils de Prud'hommes*, which were established on a city-by-city basis and pre-date the rise of modern industry.[12] Individual employment courts were established in Germany in 1890. In Britain, there were various statutory attempts to allow arbitration juries to resolve work disputes, with Acts passed to this effect in 1824, 1837 and 1872. 'It is very doubtful', however, 'whether any one of these statutes [was ever] applied in a single instance.'[13] The Employers and Workmen Act 1875 gave Courts of Summary Jurisdiction and County Courts special powers to rescind contracts, to adjust their terms, and to order specific performance in cases arising between employers and workmen involving up to £10 and in apprenticeship cases.[14] At the end of the First World War, one of the several demands to be found in the programme of the demobilised soldiers was for 'Minimum conditions in all industries to be established by law, such minimum to be a wage sufficient to maintain a family in a reasonable state of comfort, and their practical applications decided by Tribunals, consisting of Employers and Employees'.[15] Yet when the present-day Tribunals took form, as we shall see, it was not as a result of a sustained campaign from below.

Industrial Tribunals were established under the Industrial Training Act in 1964, and their first cases were heard the following year. The Act proposed to deal with the problem of unemployment by encouraging employers to train as many skilled workers as possible. This in turn was done by establishing a tripartite Central Training Council, with reserved seats for representatives of employers, unions, and of education, training and the professions.[16] Together with the Central Training Council, provision was made for the formation of Industrial Training Boards on a sector-by-sector basis. Money was levied on employers to finance the Industrial Training Boards (ITBs) and to share the cost of training between companies in each affected industry. Employers could in turn apply for grants, for example, where they sought to improve their training arrangements. Employers could appeal the decisions of the ITBs. These appeals were heard by the Industrial Tribunal.[17]

The first reported Industrial Tribunal case gives the flavour of a whole class of litigation. The Wool Training Board subjected all employers to a levy based on their total annual wage bill. The first year's levy was based on salaries paid between 6 April 1965 and 5 April 1966. One employer, Angus Rhodes and Company Limited, complained that between these two dates, it had sold all its machinery, and dismissed 124 of its previous 130 workers. In this context, the amount of levy it had to pay, £466, seemed to the company absurdly high. The Tribunal found that the business remained live. The employer continued to trade. Accordingly, the employer was subject to the levy, and the levy had been correctly calculated, 'Although we have some sympathy for the appellants in the particular circumstances of this particular case, we had, in law, no option but to dismiss the appeal.'[18]

Having been created under the Industrial Training Act to deal with just one specific set of cases, the Tribunals were soon given further powers. The first extension was as a result of the Redundancy Payments Act 1965, under which an employer was obliged to pay redundancy payments to an employee who was dismissed for reason of redundancy and who had been in continuous employment for a minimum period of two years after the age of 18, in a formula based on age up to a maximum of 20 weeks' payment. From the point of view of the employee, the law of redundancy was after 1965 relatively similar to what it is today.[19] From the point of view of the employer, however, one very significant difference was that the employer was obliged to pay contributions to a national Redundancy Fund.[20] Where the employer made redundancies, he was able to claim back a rebate from the fund. Disputes as to an award between the Secretary of State and either an employee or an employer could be referred to the Industrial Tribunal. Under the same Act, the Tribunal also acquired jurisdiction to hear cases where an employer failed to issue an employee with written particulars of employment within 13 weeks of starting employment.[21] The Tribunals acquired further jurisdictions as a result of the Selective Employment Payments Act 1966, which imposed certain taxes on employers, and the Docks and Harbour Act 1966, which empowered Tribunals to consider whether employment was dock work for purposes including the licensing of dock employment.

One 1966 survey estimated that 60 per cent of the Tribunal's recorded business was made up of appeals by employers against assessment for the industrial training levy. Yet the same source also recorded cases such as *J.C. King Ltd* v *Valencia*, in which the court was faced with deciding whether a travelling salesman was entitled to a redundancy payment. The decision boiled down to whether Mr Valencia was an employee or not. In the Tribunal's words:

> Mr Valencia agreed to enter the services of J.C. King Ltd as a selling agent. He was paid a weekly remuneration plus commission. The employers laid down fairly precise and definite terms governing what he could do and what he could not do in the course of his employment. They paid the employer's contribution for national insurance. On all these facts we think that this was a contract of service.[22]

The question of marking the precise dividing point between worker and employee remains of course a preoccupation of UK employment law, more than 40 years later.[23] It was *King* v *Valencia*, rather than the training levy cases, which pointed to the future.

Yet although the legislation concerning redundancy payments gave the Tribunal jurisdiction over claims which had a private aspect, the legislation was still equally concerned with the citizen's public law relationship with the state. One early employment lawyer, Roger Greenhalgh, describes the dynamic well:

> Although this latter class of case had the appearance of, and indeed was conducted as, a trial between two private citizens, the employee and the employer ... it had more than a trace of the citizen / state element in it. For one thing, the Secretary of State always had a right to be represented at any Tribunal hearings

> under the Redundancy Payments Act ... It could be argued that the employer, in resisting an employee's claim for a redundancy payment, was acting as the State's agent in the protection of the Redundancy Fund.[24]

If the extension of the Tribunal's jurisdiction could have been halted in (say) 1966, then the Tribunals would have been left permanently in push-me pull-you territory, as much bodies for scrutinising state administrators as civil courts.

It is often said that the plan to establish the Tribunals as the main forum to hear workplace disputes was the work of civil servants. Linda Dickens writes:

> With hindsight, one can detect the importance of the civil service thinking in the development of the present-day Industrial Tribunals. At the time the Ministry of Labour was suggesting the Tribunals might deal with all employer/employee disputes, no political party, no employer's organisation, no trade union made a central demand for new labour courts.[25]

Wedderburn echoes this narrative:

> In 1967, facing new concerns about employers' 'arbitrary' dismissals, the old National Joint Advisory Council proposed that the way ahead lay in reformed collective bargaining, but the Ministry of Labour bureaucracy sold the Tribunals to the Donovan Royal Commission as potentially 'the nucleus of a system of labour courts', in individual employment disputes ... The new dominance of legislation began in this period, not because some new discourse descended on lawyers cerebrally like the gentle rain from heaven, amidst the economic and social change, but because of the emergent economic and social change itself ... Many of us at the time not unnaturally hoped that the old liberal system, or at least its values, could be retained and adapted, especially in the sphere of collective bargaining. What we underrated was not the value of autonomous collective bargaining but the power of emergent global capital.[26]

Given the evident importance of the Donovan Commission, it is worth looking a bit more closely at how it reached the decision to recommend the extension of the Industrial Tribunals' jurisdiction. The members of the Commission included the head of the National

Coal Board (Lord Robens), the General Secretary of the TUC (George Woodcock), a former director of the British Employers' Federation (Sir George Pollock), Lord Collison of the Agricultural Workers' Union, Hugh Clegg, the sociologist of industrial relations, Mary Green, the campaigner for comprehensive education, Andrew Shonfield, Director of Studies at the Royal Institute of International Affairs and Eric Wigham, the labour editor of *The Times*. Beyond Donovan himself (a Lord Justice of Appeal and former Labour MP), there were but two other lawyers, the academic Otto Kahn-Freund, and Baron Tangley of Blackheath, a constitutional lawyer. Kahn-Freund was the only employment lawyer.

The terms of reference of the Donovan Commission made no mention of individual employment law. The Commission was invited rather

> To consider relations between management and employees and the role of trade unions and employers' associations in promoting the interests of their members and in accelerating the social and economic advance of the nation, with particular reference to the law affecting those bodies; and to report.[27]

Unsurprisingly, Donovan's first paper to the Commission emphasised industrial problems. 'What are the pros and cons of the strike weapon?', he asked, 'what are the pros and cons of the closed shop?'[28]

It was not until May 1967, by which time the Commission had been meeting for over two years, that the extension of individual employment rights was first canvassed. The author of the proposal was Otto Kahn-Freund, and the circulation of his paper was intended to pre-empt the report of the National Joint Advisory Council (NJAC), which was due to report shortly on the same issues. Perhaps sensing the direction in which the NJAC was likely to go (that is, in favour of extended collective bargaining), Kahn-Freund argued for a different solution:

> The urgency of the problem derives from the present state of the law in this country. The law protects the employee, but not against arbitrary or unfair dismissal. All he can claim is to be paid for the period of the contract or statutory notice or for the remainder of the period of a contract made for a definite period. Beyond this, he has no right, however long he may have served the employer

> and however great the hardships he suffers as the result of his dismissal. Even if the manner in which he is dismissed constitutes an imputation upon his honour and his expectation to obtain alternative employment is correspondingly reduced, he cannot, except through an action for defamation, obtain any redress.[29]

What strikes a present-day reader is the tone with which the project had to be argued. This was written advocacy. The author was trying to *persuade* the Commission, searching for the most effective arguments, knowing that his proposal did not yet have the support of the majority of Commissioners.

The purpose of the Donovan Commission was to reduce what was perceived to be the high number of unofficial strikes in Britain. Kahn-Freund bent his arguments to this cause:

> Friction caused by dismissals is a contributory and considerable cause of (mainly unofficial) strikes and other stoppages. It would be rash to predict the legislation of the kind under discussion would remove this cause of industrial unrest, but if the procedure is manifestly fair and, above all, very speedy, it can reduce the number of stoppages at least to some extent.[30]

As if just to reinforce the point, civil servants at the Ministry of Labour helpfully added at the end of the document, an appendix containing information on the causes of unofficial strikes. This showed that dismissals and suspensions were responsible for around one-eighth of all unofficial strikes. They were not the predominant cause of unofficial strikes (that was workers' use of strikes to increase their wages), but they were a significant factor (see Table 2.1).

Table 2.1 Number of unofficial strikes in 1965, by cause[31]

Cause	Number
Wages	1,173
Hours of work	22
Demarcation	59
Redundancy, dismissal, suspension	332
Working arrangements	761
Trade union recognition	28
Closed shop	32
Victimisation for union membership	13
Trade union status	8
Sympathy disputes	26
Total	2,454

Kahn-Freund's idea won over Donovan himself, who asked him to write the first draft of the section of the Report that would deal with unfair dismissals.[32] Kahn-Freund's draft, which included his proposal to extend the powers of the Industrial Tribunal, was discussed by the Commissioners on 10 October 1967. It was their 94th meeting, and the first recorded occasion on which anyone other than Kahn-Freund expressed a view as to the merits of his proposals. Kahn-Freund himself was absent. In the initial exchanges, a number of Commissioners spoke against the idea of legislation to outlaw unfair dismissal or at least against the idea that the problem should be solved primarily by legislation; from the meeting's minutes, it appears that the idea was by no means assured of progress. Yet there seems to have been little desire on the part of the Commissioners to scrap the draft entirely and begin anew. George Woodcock of the TUC argued that 'Both employers and workers would be reluctant to see a statutory body adjudicating on the merits of a particular dismissal.' Sir George Pollock of the British Employers' Federation backed Woodcock in part, saying rather that if there had to be Tribunals, they should be for other purposes, and servants (that is, employees) should not have the right to bring cases to them. Lord Robens of the National Coal Board spoke in favour of the scheme. Woodcock then attempted to make his point again. He 'said the subject matter of the Commission was industrial relations. There was no need to stray too far from this field.'[33] No vote was taken, but after this meeting and despite Woodcock's intervention, the Commissioners proceeded as if Kahn-Freund's proposal had been adopted.

At the next meeting, the Commissioners discussed the detail of the plan. Andrew Shonfield asked about the powers that the 'dismissals Tribunal' would have in relation to dismissed trade unionists. Kahn-Freund was now present, and a lengthy discussion followed, in which he spoke several times.[34] From October 1967 onwards, other members of the Commission were writing papers of their own in which the development of some form of industrial court or Tribunal was taken for granted.[35]

Along with the establishment of a system of Industrial Tribunals, the second defining feature of the Donovan Report (from the perspective of the development of today's Employment Tribunal system) was its failure to make reinstatement the primary remedy for unfair dismissals. Donovan's final Report was clear:

> Reinstatement does not offer a satisfactory solution when an employee is found to have been unfairly dismissed, because the circumstances of the dismissal have opened a permanent rift between employer and employee. In such cases, monetary compensation affords the only proper remedy.[36]

Once again we find the policy argument addressed most fully in an earlier paper written for the Commissioners by Otto Kahn-Freund:

> Whilst it would be very rash to say that an order for reinstatement and its enforcement through measures corresponding to what we call attachment or contempt of court must be entirely ruled out, the experience of foreign countries does not suggest that compulsory reinstatement is likely to be very successful. The German law, as the Committee already knows, is to the effect that on principle the court makes an order for reinstatement, but that at the option of either the employer or the employee it fixes compensation in lieu of reinstatement. The writer of this paper had considerable experience with the corresponding provisions of the previous German legislation of 1920. This was experience in a labour market situation very different from that of today, that is, during the depression of the late 20s and early 30s when it was extremely difficult for a dismissed employee to find a new job. Even so, it was the general impression of the present writer and of all those colleagues to whom he spoke, and clearly visible from the reported decisions, that in practice compensation was the order of the day. This may not be very surprising because it was the employer who had the option and inevitably he opted for compensation. But it is impossible to remember any case in which an attempt was made by the trade union to press the employer into not exercising his option for compensation, once the case had reached the court stage with which the present writer was concerned.[37]

The question of reinstatement was debated within the Commission, with attention focusing on the position of dismissed shop stewards. One shared assumption appears to have been that while dismissals in general were not a particularly important cause of strikes, dismissals of shop stewards were. In effect, members of the Commission took two positions. One group believed that there should be no remedy of reinstatement. A second group sought to keep the remedy for shop stewards. No one, however, argued for the position that reinstatement should be available as a general remedy, whenever a dismissal was found to be unfair. The following extracts from the minutes give a flavour of the discussion:

> Miss Green observed that compulsory reinstatement by law would not facilitate good industrial relations. The essence of the employer / employee relationship would already have been destroyed.
>
> Mr Shonfield replied that he did not accept. People in all walks of life had to accommodate their actions to the requirements of the law.
>
> Professor Kahn-Freund said that this generalisation did not hold true of industrial relations. Here the analogy one should have in mind was that of forcing a husband and wife to live together when they no longer wished to do so … .
>
> The Chairman asked if it should be laid down that in some circumstances the employer should have the power only to suspend and not to dismiss?
>
> Mr Wigham said that where dismissal of a trade union official was concerned the cause of industrial peace would be greatly served if the employer were only able to suspend. Furthermore, it was clearly desirable that voluntary agreements should provide wherever possible for suspension rather than dismissal.
>
> Professor Kahn-Freund pointed out that … it should be in the power of the Tribunal to make an order by which as an alternative to the payment of compensation the employer should reinstate the employee so that the latter should be deemed to have been suspended for a stated number of days. He thought this was as far as one could go.[38]

This was a chance to write a benign employment law from first principles, but the Commissioners rejected the one reform which might have helped workers most of all.

* * *

So far, the significance of the Donovan Report has been treated as residing in its advocacy of something like our present-day Tribunal system. Yet as far as most contemporaries were concerned, the key question before the Commission was rather what to do about unofficial strikes. The Report endorsed the assumption of politicians and journalists, that unofficial strikes were a destructive force in the UK economy: 'We have no hesitation in saying that the prevalence of unofficial strikes, and their tendency ... to increase, have such serious economic implications that measures to deal with them are profoundly necessary.'[39] To deal with this problem, the Commissioners made various proposals, to redefine unions as permanent combinations of workers (with the effect that where strikes were done by purely temporary combinations of workers, the strikers would be vulnerable in law for their employer's losses), to require employers and unions to negotiate factory productivity agreements and factory procedures for resolving grievances, and to create a new Industrial Relations Commission, with powers to order compulsory arbitration where unions struck in breach of these agreements. The net effect of these proposals would have been to strengthen the powers of shop stewards, both against their employers (the combined effect of the grievance procedures and the extension of the jurisdiction of the Industrial Tribunals would be to make it much harder for an employer to dismiss a trade unionist) and against their members (by giving shop stewards a say in production, it was hoped, they would also acquire responsibility for it). The Report did not call either for tortious or criminal sanctions against unofficial strikes, or even for sanctions to make agreements lawfully binding, a proposal which was being made in the press with the idea of assisting employers to sue striking unions. The public response to Donovan was for this reason almost entirely determined by the supposed 'moderation' of the Commission's proposals. The newspapers and businesses, broadly, were dissatisfied; trade union officials were relieved.

After Donovan, the next policy initiative was a Conservative Party report, *Fair Deal at Work*. This document accepted the bulk of the Donovan proposals, save that it pushed them harder in the direction of sanction. Trade unions should be required to register with a new Registrar of Trade Unions and Employers' Associations; trade unions should be capable of being sued in tort, and the Secretary of State should be able to order a 60-day compulsory cooling-off period where there were unofficial strikes. As for Tribunals, 'There would be special industrial courts comprising legally-qualified chairmen sitting with lay members from both sides of industry.'[40]

Almost immediately afterwards, the Labour Government published its own White Paper, *In Place of Strife*. The policy recommendations in this document were very close to those of *Fair Deal at Work*. Rather than a 60-day cooling-off period, only 28 days were envisaged. As for Tribunals, *In Place of Strife* recommended the formation of 'an industrial board to hear certain types of case against employers, trade unions and individual employees'.[41] Barbara Castle adopted an idea which had been rejected by the Donovan Commissioners, namely that the Tribunals should have jurisdiction over collective as well as individual disputes. Where there were unofficial strikes, the White Paper suggested, attachment of earnings orders could be made against the individual strikers involved. Popular responses to *In Place of Strife* were polarised along similar lines to responses to Donovan, except this time the positions were reversed. The press and business were enthusiastic, unions were hostile. A special TUC congress was held on 5 June 1969, voting to express its 'unalterable opposition to statutory financial penalties on work people or trade unions'.[42] Ultimately, *In Place of Strife* was dropped in favour of a TUC undertaking that its members would take internal action to prevent unofficial strikes.

Three years after the Donovan Report was published, its proposals for the extension of the jurisdiction of Industrial Tribunals finally became law, in the Industrial Relations Act 1971. By now, there was a new Conservative Government, led by Edward Heath, and the Act broadly followed *Fair Deal at Work*. A new Registrar[43] was created and unions were required to register with him. Industrial Tribunals were empowered to hear unfair dismissal cases. Individual disputes were kept separate from collective disputes, to be heard by a National Industrial Relations Court.

The enduring consequence of the Industrial Relations Act, for our purposes, is that it gave Industrial Tribunals the power to hear unfair dismissal cases. Four decades later, this remains the characteristic feature of the system, the most important type of case. A claimant who knows no law is most likely to hear the Tribunals mentioned for the first time in the context of a dismissal.

The extension of the Tribunals to hear unfair dismissal cases was, like other parts of the Act, unpopular with a majority of trade unionists. In 1961, the TUC had questioned its affiliated unions as to whether there should be legislation against unfair dismissal, 44 of the 57 unions that responded (chiefly the larger unions, representing a total of 4.6 million members) indicated their opposition to such legislation. Only 11 out of 57 (chiefly smaller unions, with a total of 225,000 members) indicated their support.[44] There was still a similar hostility ten years' later. The opposition of a majority of trade unionists to the extension of the Tribunals' power was articulated by Tony Topham of the Institute of Workers' Control:

> The Commission proposes that workers should be given the right of appeal to a Labour Tribunal ... in cases of unjust dismissal ... The burden of proof would be on the employer in such cases. But an employer can, by reason of his status ... always find reasons for a dismissal which a bourgeois court will accept as reasonable ... In crucial cases, where legal protection may be needed by victimised workers, the Tribunals would prove quite inadequate.[45]

At first sight, this opposition to the development of the Tribunals is surprising and requires explanation. The most obvious approach would be to assume that workers would benefit from the extension of their rights. Even allowing for the starting problem that workers would not be able to claim the remedy of reinstatement, surely, the overall result was a net gain. Surely, you would think, the unions should have been delighted at the extension of protection for workers against rogue employers.

Part of the explanation is that trade unions had long distrusted the British courts, doubting that they were capable of providing justice for workers. This antipathy predated the 1971 legislation, and took in the memory of cases such as Taff Vale, the judgment in 1901 which had made unions legally liable to employers for the employers' loss of business caused by strikes.[46] It was the threat posed to unions by the Taff Vale decision that had led unions to affiliate to the Labour Representation Committee which in 1906 spawned the Labour Party.[47]

By 1971, a more recent memory was the 1964 case of *Rookes v Barnard*, which concerned a draughtsman Rookes, who was dismissed by his employer, British Overseas Airways Corporation (a forerunner of today's BA). The reason for his dismissal was that he refused to be a member of the recognised union. As part of an attempt to enforce a closed shop, the union had contacted the employer warning of strikes if Rookes was not dismissed. The House of Lords turned back into history, digging up an obscure seventeenth-century civil wrong, the tort of intimidation. Finding that this relic of the law still applied, the Lords made it the centrepiece of their judgment that the union's action had been unlawful.[48] The Lords' decision appeared to have the effect that whenever a trade union proposed strike action and drew this proposal to the employer's attention, the union was intimidating the employer and committing a legal wrong and would be liable to the employer for damages.

As far as policy makers were concerned, making the fairness of dismissals a legal question rather than a trial of industrial strength would mean fewer strikes, and if the number of strikes was reduced, unions would be weakened. In the words of the White Paper that preceded the 1971 Act, 'Britain is one of the few countries where dismissals are a frequent cause of strike action. It seems reasonable to link this with the fact that in this country, unlike most others, the law provides no redress for the employee who suffers unfair or arbitrary dismissal.'[49] Such arguments had also been part of Otto Kahn-Freund's arsenal, when seeking to persuade his fellow Commissioners to expand the Tribunals, as we have seen.

* * *

The Act caused some of the most dramatic protests in recent British history. In December 1970, for example, there was a one-day strike of between 350,000 and 600,000 trade unionists opposed to the legislation. A TUC demonstration against the bill in February 1971 saw 140,000 people march. In September 1971, the TUC instructed unions not to attend hearings of the new National Industrial Relations Court (NIRC). Indirectly, the legislation was part of the story of the many disputes that took in 1971 and 1972, including the 1972 miners' strike, a work to rule on the railways, and sit-ins among Manchester engineers. Directly, it became a defining feature of the various dockers' unofficial strikes, which led five dockworkers to be jailed at Pentonville prison for contempt of court arising from their refusal to attend hearings of the NIRC. In response to their jailing, there was an unofficial strike movement on Fleet Street, in the London docks, and on building sites in central and east London which secured the release of the five dockers.[50] The government was desperate to get the dockers out of prison and end the strike wave, but the jailed workers refused to leave; the Official Solicitor, normally only appointed to take decisions on behalf of those too ill to appear in court, ordered their release. These strikes made the decisions of the National Industrial Relations Court unenforceable. It was an extraordinary moment of successful protest against the law.

While the Tribunals' right to hear dismissal cases was not at the forefront of union protests, it was part of the story. Thus, for example, as part of its opposition to the Act, the TUC instructed unions to withdraw their representatives from Tribunal panels. The Act was repealed by the Labour Government following Labour's election victory in February 1974, yet the Industrial Tribunals remained, retaining jurisdiction over unfair dismissals, and took on further powers over the next five years including under the Equal Pay Act, the Sex Discrimination and the Race Relations Acts.

By the end of the 1970s, a number of academic commentators had begun to argue that the unions' long-standing distrust of the Tribunals was misplaced.[51] As for the present, union voices opposed to the Tribunal system are rarely heard. The key voices arguing for the reduction or dismantling of the Tribunal system are those of employers. But this shift is not a sign that Tribunals produce outcomes favourable to labour. Quite the reverse, strike figures have fallen since 1971 and during the lifetime of the Tribunal system, the trade unions have been weakened. Social inequality has widened and the security of employees in post has been reduced.

* * *

In their early days, Industrial Tribunals lacked a settled infrastructure or premises. The Tribunals sometimes borrowed other courts or even council chambers for their hearings; for example:

> Sir Diarmid Conroy, [the first] President of the Industrial Tribunals ... recounts how a number of litigants withdrew their cases when they were told that they would be heard at the Royal Courts of Justice, some of whose rooms had been borrowed by the Tribunals for the purpose of hearings. The litigants had been frightened off. He also tells of an experience when he presided at a Tribunal hearing in the Council chamber of a North of England town 'from an oak throne half way up the wall'; a situation which was not conductive to putting the parties at their ease.[52]

By 1983, some 35,000 cases a year were before the Tribunal, with most concerning unfair dismissal (72.9 per cent) and redundancy payments (9.3 per cent).[53] The proportion of unfair dismissal cases has since fallen to around one in four of all Tribunal cases.[54] Among the best known of the post-1971 jurisdictions, are actions for sex, race, disability, sexual orientation, religious and age discrimination (introduced in 1975, 1976, 1993, 2003, 2003 and 2006). Meanwhile, the number of cases has in general risen, to 218,100 claims in 2010–11.[55]

* * *

'The present system of Employment Tribunals bears as much relationship' to the 1971 model, writes Patrick Elias, a past president of the Employment Appeal Tribunal and now Court of Appeal Judge,

> ... as the computer does to the calculator. The jurisdiction of Tribunals has grown massively. They now deal with law which is of very considerable complexity, as any litigant caught up in indirect discrimination claims quickly learns. The amounts of compensation are in many fields unlimited, and complex cases may take weeks to be heard.[56]

Some of this account reflects cases before the EAT better than cases before the Tribunal. The five most common categories of claim before the Tribunals in 2010–11 were unfair dismissal, wages, breach of contract, equal pay and working time claims.[57] Only the last of these would have been unfamiliar to the employment lawyer of the 1970s.

The story of the Tribunals since 1971 is in fact a history of expansion along lines which already were set. Even where there is appearance of change, this becomes less marked on close inspection. To take one example, over the past 20 years, there has been a tendency for the proportion of discrimination cases to rise, at the expense of the proportion of unfair dismissal cases. This is especially true of sex discrimination and equal pay claims. The significance of this change is discussed in Chapter 4. One reason for the shift is that discrimination claims carry higher potential remedy than ordinary unfair dismissal cases. What has changed is the labelling, rather than the substance, of the complaint.

The most significant changes have taken place outside the Tribunals. They include tendencies towards smaller workplace units, lower levels of union membership and the inexorable trend towards greater productivity and more intense working.

The real story of the past four decades has been the transition from a way of dealing with employment conflicts in which the disputes were resolved collectively, and usually outside the law, to one in which disputes are resolved most often by courts and Tribunals, and today concern individuals rather than classes of people. This story would be an optimistic one if, for example, the juridification of employment relations had resulted in a social compromise under which it was more difficult for employers to hire and fire at will. Yet the result has been the opposite. I have cited earlier the number of unfair dismissal cases that result in an order for reinstatement. Not even the most pessimistic of trade unionist, worried in 1970 or 1971 about the possible vagaries of strike action would have guessed that workers were about to consent to a new industrial order in which less than one in 6,000 contested dismissals would result in an order of reinstatement or re-engagement.

3
Agency Workers

Employment Judge: Why did you recruit security officers on agency worker contracts?

Witness for the Respondent: At that time the use and scope of pre-security checks [at airports] was under Government review and [my company] did not want to incur significant redundancy costs in the event that pre-security checks were scrapped.[1]

One in 20 workers in Britain is an agency worker.[2] The proportion here is higher than in any other country in the European Union, with the result that one in eight of all agency workers in Europe are working in Britain.[3] In the spring of 2008, before the recession which began later that year, the Reed employment agency was advertising an extraordinary 310,000 UK vacancies on its website.[4] The major employers of agency work include some of the largest private employers in Britain: such as Microsoft, Tesco and British Telecom. Agency employment is a very profitable business. In 2005, there were around 17,000 employment agencies in the UK, with an aggregate turnover of £27 billion.[5] For the workers employed in this way, the story is different. In February 2008, a TUC survey found that agency workers are paid one-fifth less than the average British worker. Only a quarter have been employed for more than a year, and half would rather be directly employed.[6]

Some of the worst-treated workers in the UK work on agency contracts. In May 2008, the Employment Appeal Tribunal (EAT) heard a case concerning a number of Polish factory and food processing workers who brought complaints against a company called Consistent Group. The workers lived in accommodation provided by the agency. They travelled to work on transport provided by the agency. They were required to pay £56.40 a week for these services. They were required to work more than 48 hours a week. They were not allowed holidays. The net effect of these deductions was that the workers were paid less than the minimum wage. When they joined a union, they were sacked. 'The [workers] were recruited in Poland', the EAT observed, 'transport and accommodation was provided in circumstances where they were not in reality in a position to refuse them, and there were severe practical and legal limits placed on their working elsewhere whilst the contract with the agency was maintained.'[7]

Of course, not all agency workers face compulsion on this scale. The category of agency worker is wide enough to comprise at one end well-paid telecommunication specialists[8] and chartered accountants.[9] At the other end, very many agency workers are labourers, factory hands, or other unskilled workers. This disparity helps to explain why, for example, *only* half of the agency workers interviewed for the TUC survey would have preferred direct employment.

For many years, unions campaigned for measures to equalise the pay and conditions of agency workers, focusing especially on the plight of casual and migrant agency workers. Their model was the legislation prohibiting discrimination against workers on part-time or fixed-term contracts.[10] This campaign reached a first high point in July 2004, in the aftermath of the invasion of Iraq, when an isolated Labour Cabinet with an eye on the approaching General Election accepted the need to legislate for agency workers as one of the terms of its Warwick Agreement with the unions. Under the same agreement, the Cabinet also agreed a range of policies which would have a wide impact across industry: the Cabinet pledged to protect pensions for workers moving from one employer to another, to promote sector forums in areas of low-paid work, as well as to limit the employer's right to dismiss strikers in the first twelve weeks of their employment.[11]

For months, the pledge to protect agency workers remained on the table. Labour did not implement its promise, nor did it resile from it. Two things ultimately changed. First, a series of decisions by the Tribunal (and especially the EAT) had the effect of reducing the rights of agency workers dramatically and therefore pushing the issue of agency workers back up the policy agenda. Secondly, through 2007 and 2008, pressure came from the European Union for legislation. Not for the first time in the recent history of United Kingdom labour law, a positive measure was adopted in order to comply with European standards. Yet the measure adopted is modest and will not advance workers' rights. It would not have been needed but for the decisions of the employment courts. Indeed, those judgments continue to have an effect; the European legislation will help only at the margins.

PUSHING RIGHTS BACKWARDS?

The most basic protection in UK employment law is the right to claim unfair dismissal. Every other right is contingent on it. To give a familiar example, consider an employee who is bullied by their manager at work. The employee has the right to resign and bring an action for unfair constructive dismissal. Sometimes, the mere mention of the threat will be enough to concentrate the mind of the employer. A more senior manager may warn the bully to stop. But if a worker knows that they will not be able to bring an action for unfair dismissal, the threat of the sanction is less. Probably, they will not complain; in all likelihood, the bullying will continue.

When any worker brings a case to an Employment Tribunal, one of the first questions facing a Tribunal is the worker's employment status. By operation of section 94(1) of the Employment Rights Act 1996 ('an employee has the right not to be unfairly dismissed by his employer'), only employees and no other groups of workers are entitled to bring unfair dismissal claims. The reasons for this distinction are historic. As UK employment law was formulated, a discrete policy decision was taken that the law should protect only employees (or, in the older terminology, 'servants').[12] Other groups of workers, it was determined, did not need protection. Now, over time, this distinction has been blurred, not least because European employment law normally extends its protection to workers, who are a wider group of people.[13] But from the perspective of the Tribunal, it is necessary to distinguish workers and employees. If a statute specifically refers to employees, then it is assumed that the statute protects only employees and not all workers. As for the meaning of these terms, everyone at work is a 'worker': the category is large enough to include directors of companies and people running businesses where they are the sole worker. The Employment Rights Act defines an employee as a person working under a contract of employment.[14] Case law in turn defines an employment contract as a contract in which a worker works under an employer's control.[15]

Absent the right to bring an unfair dismissal claim and all other workplace rights are diminished. A worker, who is not an employee, may bring a claim of unlawful deduction of wages against an employer, and because the right to wages is extended to all workers,[16] she may succeed. But if the employer dismisses the worker in retaliation, the worker will not be able to succeed with a claim of unfair dismissal.[17] The losses of the dismissed worker in these circumstances are in practice far greater than the benefits of their potential claim. For this reason, most non-employees do not bring unlawful deduction claims, or even raise them with their employers as complaints. The complaints are not worth the risk of dismissal.

To some limited extent, the distinction between workers and employees makes a certain sense. If an employer who runs his own business goes bankrupt, and stops working for that company, it must be right that he or she cannot normally sue the company for unfair dismissal. The employer could hardly sue him- or herself for damages. Likewise, it is right that a very highly paid self-employed consultant working for the National Health Service, who has a high degree of bargaining power in choosing the terms of their engagement, is treated differently from, say, an employee on a standard contract of employment, who has radically less power to control the terms of their work. But where this distinction is applied to agency workers, it is unhelpful. Agencies, as employment businesses, are required by law to give agency workers a written contract setting out the terms under which the workers are engaged.[18] Typical agency contracts label the worker a self-employed contractor. There is no more thinking to this process than a desire, on the part of companies, to evade their legal liabilities. While a directly employed worker aware of their rights might in theory protest at this device (even this would require an employee of unusual self-confidence), agency workers are by definition insecure in their rights and even less likely than their directly employed counterparts to request changes to an employment contract offered to them in standard terms.

Agency workers are the most numerous group of worker to have had difficulty in establishing their employment status, but they are not the only category of worker to have difficulty. Casual workers, freelancers, interns, volunteers,[19] and those without immigration status[20] are susceptible to the same difficulty, while many of the reported cases concern majority shareholders (who in recent years the Tribunals have tended to find *are* employees of any particular company).[21]

Another difficulty for agency workers is that there are three people in the work relationship. Agency workers fit awkwardly into common law contractual theory, which always has difficulty with tripartite relationships.[22] The agency worker will usually sign a contract to provide services through the agency. There is usually also an agreement between the agency and its client (the 'end-user'). There is rarely a contract between worker and end-user. Even assuming that an agency worker was found ultimately to be in an employment relationship, the difficulties do not end there. Which of the companies is her employer; is it the agency or the end-user? In the absence of clear facts pointing to the contrary, should there be a presumption that either the agency or the end-user is normally the employer? When should a contract be deemed formed: immediately, after a year, or after some other time? In a context where there is no statutory provision giving clear answers to these questions, the courts have had to provide answers of their own.

In 2004, the Court of Appeal heard the case of *Dacas* v *Brook Street*; which concerned Ms Dacas, a cleaner who had worked for four years at a local authority-run mental hostel, via an agency, Brook Street. She was found by the Tribunal to be an employee of neither the agency nor the Council. She appealed, for reasons which are not clear, only against the finding that she was not an employee of the agency. The three Judges in the Court of Appeal saw the case in different terms from each other, but a majority (Lord Justices Mummery and Sedley) determined that Ms Dacas was an employee, and that she had been employed not by the agency but by the Council. The concern which weighed heaviest on the Court of Appeal was the length of time for which Ms Dacas had been employed. Lord Justice Mummery suggested that when cases of this nature came before Tribunals in future, agency workers on long-term placements should normally be found to be employees:

> The first impression gained, on looking at the practical realities of the triangular arrangement, is that the applicant is more likely to be regarded as an employee of the end-user than as an employee of the employment agency or as not being an employee at all. There is no dispute in cases like the present that the applicant has done work for the end-user at the end-user's premises and under the control of the end-user.[23]

Lord Justice Sedley compared Ms Dacas' situation to that of an ordinary employee working for an employer without a written contract. In this case, the Council argued that it could not be her employer, as it had never provided her with a contract of employment. However, an ordinary worker, in this typical situation, also might not have a written contract; the absence would not stop a court from finding a contract implied.[24] While the decision offered nothing to benefit Ms Dacas herself (she had not pursued her appeal against the Council), it did open a route for others to bring claims.

In 2005 and 2006, the EAT and the Court of Appeal heard a second agency worker case, this time involving a Mr Muscat, who was a well-paid computer specialist. He had originally been employed by a company, EIL, but was placed on a consultancy contract by the company (as part of a discrete process by which the employer made itself attractive for take-over by moving its workers from written employment contracts to contracts in which they were termed 'consultants', and therefore made its payroll seem lower than it was). EIL was in due course taken over by Cable & Wireless, who required Mr Muscat to provide his services via an agency. The Court of Appeal had no difficulty in finding that Muscat was an employee of Cable & Wireless. In doing so, it made a brief, passing reference to an older case, *The Aramis*,[25] in which it had been said that (in general) a contract may only be implied into being where it is 'necessary' to do so. This, the Court said, had been the logic of the decision in *Dacas*.[26] The Court confirmed that the decision in *Dacas* had been correct, and that Mr Muscat had been an employee of Cable & Wireless.

If the matter had ended there, the law would have been clear and relatively benign. Agency workers could be employees; whether a Tribunal found that they were employees or not would depend on all the facts of the situation. Just nine months later, however, a third case changed the law very dramatically for the worse.

In December 2006, the then president of the EAT, the Honourable Mr Justice Elias[27] heard the case of *James* v *London Borough of Greenwich*,[28] which concerned Ms James, a support worker who had worked in Greenwich Council's asylum team for three years. It is nowhere quite stated directly in his judgment but it appears Elias was persuaded that in itself the agency relationship was a bona fide relationship between three parties, who had alike chosen the relationship, and that where an agency agreement existed and it had extinguished the employment status of the agency workers, this agreement was by definition robust. The following was his discussion of the point made in *Dacas* that an agency worker who had worked for the same end-user on a lengthy contract would probably be an employee:

> It will no doubt frequently be convenient for the agency to send the same worker to the end user, who in turn would prefer someone who has proved to be able and understands and has experience of the systems in operation. Many workers would also find it advantageous to work in the same environment regularly, at least if they have found it convivial. So the mere fact that the arrangements carry on for a long time may be wholly explicable by considerations of convenience for all parties; it is not necessary to imply a contract to explain the fact that the relationship has continued perhaps for a very extensive period of time. Effluxion

> of time does not of itself establish any mutual undertaking of legal obligations between the worker and end user. This is so even where the arrangement was initially expected to be temporary only but has in fact continued longer than expected. Something more is required to establish that the tripartite agency analysis no longer holds good.[29]

Elias's suggestion was that the agency worker is quite regularly being contacted by the agency with a range of alternative employment choices; from convenience, however, she turns down these repeated offers and remains in the post. In reality, her decision to remain in the role is not a matter of choice. Such a worker will not be receiving a range of offers from the agency; probably, she will have had no contact from the agency since starting the post. She remains, because this is her work. If she fails to attend at work on any particular day, she will be disciplined by either the agency (who may refuse to find her another role) or the end-user, or both.

Mr Justice Elias's conclusion was that agency workers are not employees. 'In a tripartite relationship of this kind', he held, 'the end user is not paying directly for the work done by the worker, but rather for the services supplied by the agency.'[30] When an employer recruits an employee, in other words, usually the employer associates the employee with some skill or potential which is of value to the company. But when an employer asks an agency to provide workers, there is a different relationship. In Elias's thinking, it is a matter of utter indifference to the employer whether the agency supplies a skilled worker who has been based in that company and that particular role for years, or a novice on her first day of paid work.

'The key feature', Elias continued, 'is not just the fact that the end user is not paying the wages, but that he cannot insist on the agency providing the particular worker at all.' It followed that:

> Provided the arrangements are genuine and the actual relationship is consistent with them, it is not then necessary to explain the provision of the worker's services or the fact of payment to the worker by some contract between the end user and the worker, even if such a contract would also not be inconsistent with the relationship. The express contracts themselves both explain and are consistent with the nature of the relationship and no further implied contract is justified.[31]

We are on the terrain of common law,[32] with its deep-held assumption that written contracts are to be held sacred. The employer's intention in making the agreement is to buy labour in general, rather than a particular worker. This is the offer, which the worker accepts. If the worker strikes a bad bargain, it is her mistake.

Elias's decision was that the status of an agency worker should be determined by looking chiefly at the words of the contract under which the worker was engaged. Following *The Aramis* (cited by the Court of Appeal in *Muscat* as we have seen), the contract could be disregarded only where it was 'necessary' to do so. In effect, *James* has established a new rule that only in extraordinary circumstances should the Tribunal go behind a contract labelling an agency worker as a non-employee.

The Court of Appeal upheld the EAT's decision in *James*. Lord Justice Mummery gave the leading judgment. He barely discussed the rightness or wrongness of the EAT's decision. Neither did Lord Justice Mummery acknowledge that in practice Elias had moved the test from one of where the finding of employee status (or not) were equal possibilities, to one where the finding of status is so unusual as to be worthy of comment, when it happens. He did just say this:

> As an appeal from the decision of an ET only lies on a question of law, my view is that, in general, it would be very unusual for an appeal to the EAT or to this court to have a real prospect of success if the ET's conclusion that a contract of employment with the end user should, or should not, be implied, has been reached by applying the correct test of necessity, as explained by Elias J in the judgment of the EAT and in the judgments of this court in this and other cases ... The increasing amounts of money, time and effort spent on litigating this issue in tribunals and on appeals might in some cases be invested more productively in making representations to and through bodies which can pursue the debate on policy or even reform the law.[33]

While on the face of it, this appears to be an even-handed statement to the effect that lawyers should leave this matter to the Tribunal and leave the appeal courts alone; it has been taken by the courts as a strong indicator that Elias's analysis was right.

Of the ten agency worker decisions that went to appeal between December 2007 (that is, the EAT decision in *James*) and December 2009, all ten resulted in findings that the agency worker was not an employee; and although there are no figures for ET cases themselves, the best guess is that nine out of ten or more agency worker cases presently end in findings that the agency worker lacked employee status.[34] The practical effect of this ruling has been almost the same as if agency workers had simply lost altogether the right to complain of unfair dismissal. In Britain, they are by far the largest group of workers to be deprived of that right.

PARLIAMENT

Mr Justice Elias ended his decision in *James* by calling on Parliament to legislate to protect agency workers from what even he described as the employers' 'abuse' of their economic power:

> We should not leave this case without repeating the observations made by many courts in the past that many agency workers are highly vulnerable and need to be protected from the abuse of economic power by the end users ... A careful analysis of both the problems and the solutions, with legislative protection where necessary, is urgently required.[35]

Parliament was to have several opportunities over the next few years to show how much these words were worth.

Yet before coming on to Parliament's record, it is worth explaining something more by way of context. While the judges and Parliament took an interest in agency workers' rights, they were not the only institutions to do so. The European Commission had first proposed a draft Directive to protect temporary agency workers as long ago as 1982, although the proposal was not adopted. In 1990, the Commission proposed legislation in three areas: part-time work, fixed-term contracts and temporary work. Employers' and workers' representatives reached agreement in the areas of part-time work and fixed-term contracts, which were formalised as EU Directives in 1997 and 1999 respectively. In May 2000, European unions and employers' organisations launched talks on a temporary work agreement, but these petered out after a year of negotiations. In 2002, the European Commission put forward its own proposal for a Temporary Agency Work Directive. The Finnish and then Portuguese EU presidencies of 2006 and 2007 both saw attempts to revive these proposals, which were opposed by Britain and Germany.[36] These European discussions were widely reported in the press at every stage, with the unions lobbying ministers to accept the Directive and the CBI briefing ministers against.

In 2007, Labour backbencher Paul Farrelly was successful in the private members' ballot, enabling him to move a Bill of his choice. He chose the protection of agency workers. His Bill was supported by seven of the largest unions in the country. Their active support ensured that around a hundred Labour MPs were in attendance for the Bill's second reading in March of that year. Proposing his Bill, Farrelly spoke the words necessary to placate New Labour: 'This Bill is not about regulating flexibility out of the economy. It is not anti-business.' He reminded his fellow MPs that the Government had promised legislation. A Labour frontbencher, Anne Snelgrove, rose to confirm that legislation to protect agency workers had indeed been part of the Warwick Agreement and to the best of her knowledge remained Government policy.

Jim Fitzpatrick (previously a left-wing activist in the Fire Brigades Union, now a Blairite and a junior minister at the Department of Trade and Industry) spoke against:

> I hear what my hon. Friend says. I certainly agree that there are some unscrupulous employers out there. They are not restricted to agency worker employers – some employers who are regarded as mainstream also undermine and take advantage of workers' rights.
>
> When agencies undermine people's rights, they tarnish the reputation of the whole industry and undermine decent agencies for temporary and agency workers that are doing the right thing in trying to ensure that their recruits are treated favourably. I accept that there are problems but I emphasise that we have an inspectorate, we investigate complaints and, if my hon. Friend has information and details about cases, I am happy to ensure that the appropriate officials receive them.

Fitzpatrick said that there was already a Government consultation on the rights of agency workers and hinted that this would solve all the outstanding problems. There was indeed a consultation ongoing at the time, but the reforms proposed in it were a relaxation of employment agencies' already light duties where they were supplying workers for very short-term tasks; and a ban on agencies charging fees to entertainers and models.[37] None of this would be any help to most agency workers seeking to defend their rights at work. To groans from his fellow Labour MPs, Fitzpatrick spoke on and on until he had succeeded in talking the Bill out.[38]

EUROPE

Finally, in 2008, the Labour Government accepted the need for action. It shifted its position in Europe from opposition to a Directive, to support. Shortly afterwards, an agreement was reached between the CBI and the TUC (under active government sponsorship)[39] on a formula that would protect agency workers in the following terms. Agency workers would have the same rights as directly employed workers. They would establish these rights by a comparative exercise, familiar from discrimination law. In other words, agency worker A would say that she was paid less than directly employed worker B, and that the reason for the different treatment was her agency worker status. Where agency worker A had been employed for twelve weeks, and where the Tribunal accepted that she was on worse terms that a directly employed worker, and that the reason was agency status, the worker would receive compensation.[40]

Article 5(1) of Directive 2008/104/EC on temporary agency work, which was adopted by the European Union later in 2008, now states that 'The basic working and employment conditions of temporary agency workers shall be, for the duration of their assignment at a user undertaking, at least those that would apply if they had been recruited directly by that undertaking to occupy the same job.'

The Directive is given effect in the UK by Regulations, which follow the same pattern of requiring equality of treatment between agency workers and directly employed workers in their basic working and employment conditions, defined as pay, working time, night working, rest periods, rest breaks and annual leave. The agency worker acquires these rights on completion of a qualifying period of twelve weeks. There are also provisions to prevent the avoidance of these requirements by abuse of the qualifying period.[41] The Regulations come into effect on 1 October 2011.

On arrival into office, the Conservatives sought advice as to whether it would be possible to withdraw the Regulations, or significantly diminish the protections in them. Eventually, in October 2010, Ed Davey, the Parliamentary Under-Secretary of State for Business, Innovation and Skills made a written statement to Parliament:

> ... the Government's ability to make changes to address such matters is constrained by the fact that the regulations are based

> to a significant degree on the agreement brokered by the previous Administration between the CBI and TUC. Due to this unique legal situation, any amendments proposed to the regulations touching upon the subject matter of the CBI and TUC agreement, which did not have the agreement of those parties, would face the risk of being set aside in the courts in the event of a legal challenge.

Davey went on to explain that the Government would therefore not be proceeding with any amendment of the Regulations themselves.[42]

It is possible to envisage circumstances where the new rights will be a boon. They will protect workers, for example, in a situation where a company clearly and explicitly offers worse pay or other conditions to agency workers. Equally, they will protect agency workers from other forms of differential treatment, for example, shorter rest breaks. Unfortunately, the comparative logic of the exercise means that in many other situations an agency worker will gain less than might be hoped from the legislation. If, for example, an employer recruits only agency workers and pays them very poorly, there would be no directly employed comparator on whom the agency workers could rely. The same negative result will occur also if an agency worker is made redundant in contrast to a directly employed worker who is kept on by the employer. In this situation, as a result of *James*, the agency worker will be unable to bring a claim of unfair dismissal; nothing in the Regulations protects her.[43] *James* continued to have effect in the most common situation of all, where an agency worker is dismissed and the dismissal is simply and ordinarily unfair.

The Department of Business, Innovation and Skills consulted on Regulations to implement the Directive; while it was at least *possible* that the UK's adoption of the policy set out in the Directive might have conferred protection against unfair dismissals, the single reference to the problem of employment status in the consultation document closed off even that residual hope:

> Whilst it is intended that the implementing Regulations will ensure the better protection of agency workers by ensuring the principle of equal treatment relating to basic working and employment conditions is applied to them, *it is not intended that these will formally change the current employment status of such workers*

or their entitlement to existing rights, such as the right to claim unfair dismissal.[44]

The result of the decision in *James*, unremedied as it is by the Directive or the Regulations, is a bad outcome in law for many of Britain's most vulnerable workers who have lost the most basic protection of our employment law. Politicians deserve some of the criticism, but the real defeat occurred in the employment courts.

4
Equal Pay

Apart from the fact that you've got more equality than you ever can deal with, the fact of the matter is that you've got real democracy and there really are no glass ceilings, despite the fact that some of you moan about it all the time ... Women can get to the top of any single job that they want to in the UK ...

I mean what else do you want, for God's sake? Women astronauts. Women miners. Women dentists. Women doctors. Women managing directors. What is it you haven't got?[1]

Women are still paid, on average, 22.6 per cent less per hour than men. Although this has fallen from 27.5 per cent over the last 10 years we are noticing that progress is stalling, and the number has even risen slightly since 2007, when it was 21.9 per cent. This is also the case for the full-time gender pay gap, which stood at 12.5 per cent in 2007 but is now 12.8 per cent. Pay gaps are even greater for part-time workers (39.9 per cent).[2]

One feature of employment litigation in the past five years has been the changing nature of the cases heard by Employment Tribunals. Until recently, by far the largest group of Tribunal cases was made up of claims for unfair dismissal. It is still the case that when people are trained for the first time in employment law, whether on the Bar Professional Training Course, the (solicitors') Legal Practice Course, by trade unions, or by other specialist organisations such as the Free Representation Unit, the emphasis is on unfair dismissal claims, and the assumption is that dismissals are the type of case with which any representative will deal most frequently. Representatives cut their teeth on unfair dismissals and built up to discrimination cases, which are rightly seen as more difficult. But while most people assume that Tribunals are *all* about dismissals, the content of Tribunal cases is changing. In 2006–07, for the first time, more gender discrimination claims (in other words, both sex discrimination and equal pay cases) were submitted to the Tribunal than unfair dismissal claims. This remained the picture up to 2009–10, when unfair dismissal claims again overtook gender discrimination cases, albeit narrowly (see Table 4.1). This chapter asks simply *why* have the numbers of gender discrimination claims increased in recent years?

Table 4.1 Claims (select jurisdictions), 2005–06 to 2009–10[3]

	2005–06	*2006–07*	*2007–08*	*2008–09*	*2009–10*
Total claims accepted	115,039	132,577	189,303	151,028	236,100
Unfair dismissal claims	41,832	44,491	40,941	52,711	57,400
Sex discrimination claims	14,250	28,153	26,907	18,637	18,200
Equal pay claims	17,268	44,013	62,706	45,748	37,400

It would be natural to assume that where there has been a sharp increase in the number of gender discrimination cases, logically, this transformation must be the consequence of some underlying change in the relationships between men and women at work. Yet, on any of the obvious markers of gender inequality, there has in fact been no significant worsening in the past few years. The gap between women's median hourly pay and men's has narrowed slightly in recent years, falling from 12.8 per cent in April 2006 to 10.2 per cent in April 2010.[4] In the recession that began in 2008, both men and women suffered redundancy. Yet because of the nature of the recession, its impact was felt first in sectors in which male employment has historically been higher (such as construction or manufacturing) with the result that the fall in employment rates was at first faster among men than women. Between 30 April 2008 and 30 April 2009, the total number of men in employment fell by 314,000, while total female employment fell by 84,000 (although the dramatic public sector cuts since the spring of 2011 are likely to hit women far harder than men).[5] While it remains the case that more men are still in work than women, the employment gap between the genders has narrowed in recent years, and the trend is for it to narrow further.

Concentrating just on pay; there are problems with the way in which the pay gap is calculated. The comparison between male and female hourly pay is based on a comparison of the earnings of male and female full-time workers. Part-time workers are excluded. Now, in the most general terms, some of the reasons women are paid less than men are as follows. Women suffer from 'sticky floors' (that is, on appointment, they tend to be placed in lower paid roles than similarly qualified men) and 'glass ceilings' (in the private sector especially, the very top jobs are often in practice reserved for men; of the hundred wealthiest companies in the United Kingdom, 22 still did not have a single women director in 2009).[6] There is a pregnancy-related pay gap: women leave jobs in their twenties or thirties; when they return, they often come back to part-time roles from which promotion is less likely. Where a career is seen as 'women's work' it tends to be paid less well than equivalent careers dominated by men. Some of these processes are reflected in the pay gap, others are not. For the purpose of calculating the pay gap, the figures compare a woman and a man when both are starting in a career in their twenties; if, however, the woman has a child and is absent from work and unpaid in her mid-thirties, she drops out of the statistics altogether. In particular, the pay gap fails to record the inequality women suffer as a result of them working for longer periods of part-time work.

In some sectors of the economy, gender pay inequality is connected to pay inequality between full-time and part-time workers. In higher education, for example, the majority of part-time lecturers are women, while the majority of full-time lecturers are men. The reasons for this are not simply down to pregnancy career breaks. It is also the case that men are appointed to full-time jobs earlier in their careers. Full-time lecturers are on pay scales negotiated by unions nationally. Very few full-time lecturers are paid less than the UK's national average wage of £24,000. Hourly-paid lecturers by contrast are commonly paid an hourly rate of £50 per hour or so for a 20-week teaching year. Marking and other duties are subsumed within this rate. In practice, a part-time lecturer earns about a third to a quarter of as much, per hour of teaching delivered to students, as a full-time lecturer. Thus while the 'headline' pay gap in the sector is only 16 per cent (in other words, a little but not dramatically worse than the UK average), the gap between male and female pension settlements on retirement is around 30 per cent, and since pensions are calculated in relationship to the amount of pay actually earned by any lecturer over his or her whole career, this is a much more accurate indicator of the real, career pay gap.[7]

Yet even when these concealed dynamics of equal pay are taken into account, there is no compelling evidence that women's situation in the workplace has declined markedly in recent years; more accurately, the big picture is of a glacially slow convergence between men and women in terms of pay, seniority and so on.

If the recent increase in the number of equal pay cases cannot be explained in terms of an underlying trend towards greater economic or social inequality, it might alternatively be explained as a consequence of women's changing consciousness: as a sort of 'delayed reaction' to decades of unequal pay, brought on by the growing realisation of women's subordination at work. But even an explanation of this sort would be unconvincing. If women had a more radical consciousness, it would not be apparent only before the Employment Tribunal. Yet this is not the early 1960s in the United States or the early 1970s in Britain; the politics of women's liberation is not in the ascendancy; politically, we are still stuck in a 'backlash' moment.[8]

Moreover, the law itself, both on equal pay and even on sex discrimination, has not changed dramatically during the past decade. There are other areas of discrimination law which have changed beyond any recognition over the past decade. For example, discrimination on grounds of religion or belief or on grounds of sexual orientation or on grounds of age were both made unlawful only by regulations published as recently as 2003 (religion and sexual orientation) and 2006 (age); while the case law on disability discrimination has in the same period been pushed very dramatically first one way towards the claimant,[9] and then back in the opposite direction[10] as a result of high-profile decisions of the House of Lords.

Equal pay law has changed in much more modest ways: the courts have shown a greater willingness to allow hypothetical comparators in a narrowly limited band of cases;[11] in another case, the Tribunals have found that where a woman brings a successful equal pay claim, a low-paid male colleague can 'piggy-back' with an equal pay claim of his own.[12] Against these genuine advances, there have been a number of decisions which have had the effect of narrowing workers' ability to claim. The EAT has ruled that a claimant in an equal pay case could not compare herself with a better-paid successor.[13] The appeal courts have reminded the Tribunals that equal pay will only be proven where it is found that the cause of the pay difference was indeed gender.[14] In a surprising ruling, the House of Lords found that the six-month time limit for bringing an equal pay case begins to run from the moment of a business transfer (the surprise of this decision is that it splits in two a worker's employment with a transferor and a transferee, when for all other employment law purposes, these are treated as one period of continuous employment).[15]

As for sex discrimination law, in *B* v *A*,[16] the Employment Appeal Tribunal held that the dismissal of a woman by her employer with whom she was having a relationship because he discovered she was also having a relationship with another man was not sex discrimination. The reason for dismissal, the EAT held, was the employer's jealousy, which was a gender-neutral phenomenon. The decision was controversial. The EAT should have asked itself simply whether the claimant would have been dismissed if she was a man; surely, she would not have been. Some of the harm done in *B* v *A* was remedied by the successful judicial review brought by the Equal Opportunities Commission (EOC) in 2007, which challenged proposed regulations to bring the Sex Discrimination Act in line with European law.[17] The EOC argued successfully that the regulations did not go far enough, with the result that further regulations had to be published in 2008,[18] and these confirmed that no comparator is needed in pregnancy discrimination cases,[19] as well as changing the definition of unlawful sexual harassment from conduct done 'on grounds of' sex, to conduct 'related to' sex,[20] a measure intended to reverse the decision in *B* v *A*.

Seen in the round, the development of equal pay law and sex discrimination in the past few years does not amount to a continuous pattern of reform. There have been some changes, some of which do make it slightly easier for claimants to succeed in these categories of case, but the positive changes are relatively minor and are wholly insufficient to explain the big rise in gender discrimination claims.

EQUAL PAY AND SEX DISCRIMINATION: THE LAW

Before coming to a more convincing explanation for the increased numbers of equal pay and sex discrimination cases, it is worth summarising the law. Equal pay law is derived from the Equal Pay Act 1970 and is now enshrined in sections 64–71 of the Equality Act 2010. The 2010 Act inserts into every employment contract a clause ('the sex equality clause') equalising the terms of men and women workers. If there is an unequal term by which a worker is paid less than a comparator of the opposite gender, the unequal term is overridden by the equality clause. There are three circumstances where the clause takes effect: (i) 'like work', that is, where the claimant's work is the same or of a broadly similar nature as the comparator's work and there are no important differences; (ii) 'work rated as equivalent', that is, work rated as equivalent in a job evaluation scheme; and (iii), 'work of equal value', that is, work of equal effort and skill, with the same level of decision making and so on.[21]

Where a claimant has sufficient continuous service, equal pay claims can be brought with reference to a total period of up to six years. They must be brought within six months[22] of the last payment about which the claimant complains. Claims can be brought where the claimant and the comparator are employed by different employers, but only where the source of the pay inequality is a single source (for example, both groups of workers are on the same scale, or where there is a single body that could remedy the pay disadvantage).[23] Claimants must show that there is a single factor, tainted by sex discrimination which explains the pay difference. Employers can defend equal pay cases by relying on a 'genuine material factor' untainted by pay, which explains the difference. Examples of scenarios which the courts have accepted were untainted by discrimination include where male employees were paid more because their jobs had greater responsibility,[24] or because they had more experience,[25] or their jobs involved greater physical effort,[26] or where the source of the pay differences were performance, attendance, or wet weather bonuses.[27]

The development of equal pay law has very largely been the work of the equality provisions of the European Treaty itself (article 141), of the European Directive on equal pay (1975/117) and of the European courts. Under European law, any Directives of the European Union are binding on the national governments of signatory states. What this means in practice is that where European law offers greater rights, UK public sector workers (whose employer is the government) may claim, relying not on the UK statute but on the European Directive. Over time, this has tended to result in the progressive development of equal pay law, not so much because of some generosity of the common law, but because of the purposive attitude which European judges take towards the rights set out in EU law.[28]

Although the number of equal pay cases is very high, in fact, they take up only a small proportion of the total workload of the Tribunal. For example in 2010–11, there were only 277 equal pay cases disposed of by the Tribunal, in contrast to the 37,400 claims brought by individual equal pay claimants.[29] One reason for this disparity is that equal pay cases are typically joint claims by often large numbers of workers. For example, one high-profile equal pay claim in 2006–07, which was subject to various appeals to the higher courts, involved twelve test case women claiming equal pay with two male comparators said to be doing work of equal value. 'Directly or indirectly', the Employment Appeal Tribunal noted, 'this case affects 1,500 workers.'[30] So while it is not unusual for several hundred workers to launch a joint equal pay claim, even such 'giant' claims are managed by the Tribunal and treated as if they were single cases involving a few joined claimants. The total amount of Tribunal time given over to equal pay claims remains relatively low.

By contrast, it is much rarer for wages cases or claims of unfair dismissal to be joined. This is largely a matter of practicality. Wages and unfair dismissal cases are typically brought by dismissed former employees. The facts which gave rise to joined wages or dismissal cases tend by their nature to restrict the cases to perhaps two or three claimants, rather than several hundred. Here are two cases I have dealt with:

> Case 1: A group of construction workers were ordered by the manager of the business to work for longer hours without any pay rise. They protested to their foreman, further complaining that they were being paid the wrong contractual rate for the job. The manager entered the site and dismissed two of the workers on the spot. The two workers began unfair dismissal claims separately, before later applying to have them joined.
>
> Case 2: Over a period of months if not years, a pub in London would repeatedly employ its bar staff for a month or two and then stop paying them. The workers would leave soon after. One former bartender brought a wages claim against the pub. The pub owners kept their pub shut in the day and refused to accept any post, including correspondence from solicitors or the courts. When the former bartender went back to the pub seeking payment she asked her replacement what was going on. Soon after, the replacement herself stopped being paid and brought her own wages case. The claims were joined.

Equal pay cases, in contrast to unlawful deduction of wages and unfair dismissal claims, are usually brought by people who remain working in the same job. Claimants have the chance to meet at work and discuss their plans for litigation together. Moreover, the rules on time limits make it easier to join equal pay claims. In general, a claimant must bring a claim within three months of the last act about which she complains. In case 2, above, had the pub paid its employees normally for four to five months before stopping their pay, then it is very unlikely that any one claimant would have known about the other claimant's case, and in all probability the two claims would never have been joined. Because, in equal pay cases, the complaint concerns an ongoing reduction of pay, it is possible to delay commencing an equal pay claim until relatively large numbers of claimants have signed up.

One way in which equal pay law can usefully be seen is as a particular subset of sex discrimination case, in other words, an indirect sex discrimination claim where the complaint concerns remuneration. As the description suggests, there are many other examples of sex discrimination claims: claims of harassment (where the worker is subject to unwanted conduct which violates her dignity or creates an intimidating, hostile, degrading, humiliating, or offensive environment for her), claims of direct discrimination (less favourable treatment on the grounds of sex), claims of indirect discrimination unrelated to pay (where the employer applies to a worker a provision, criterion or practice which puts or would put the worker at a particular disadvantage compared to a worker of the opposite gender and which the employer cannot show to be a proportionate means of achieving a legitimate aim), and victimisation (where a worker is subject to a detriment for having brought her own or supported another worker's allegation of sex discrimination). A worker must bring one of these complaints within three months of the last act about which she complains, although this limit can be extended where it would be just and equitable to do so.

In sex discrimination cases, claimants are potentially entitled to a wider set of remedies than they are in wages or unfair discrimination cases. So, for example, as a result of a very old common law case which long precedes the establishment of the Employment Tribunals,[31] a worker in a 'standard' unfair dismissal case has no remedy for any distress caused to them by the events of their dismissal. This position can be contrasted to the situation of a claimant in a discrimination case, who potentially can claim damages for injury to feelings caused to them by a discriminatory act (including a discriminatory dismissal).[32] In addition, while the compensatory element of the remedy for an unfair dismissal is ordinarily capped (as of 1 February 2011, the cap was £68,400),[33] where a dismissal is unfair because it was done for a discriminatory reason the cap does not apply. Advantages such as these may help to explain the general trend for the total number of all discrimination cases to rise, both absolutely and in proportion to unfair dismissal claims (see Table 4.2).

While the advantages of discrimination over dismissal claims does not explain the trend towards increased equal pay claims, it may help to explain why more sex discrimination cases are being brought now than in the middle of the last decade.

Table 4.2 Claims (on grounds of discrimination), 2005–06 to 2009–10[34]

	2005–06	*2006–07*	*2007–08*	*2008–09*	*2009–10*
Sex	14,250	28,153	26,907	18,637	18,200
Sexual orientation	395	470	582	600	710
Disability	4,585	5,533	5,833	6,578	7,500
Age	n/a	972	2,949	3,801	5,200
Race	4,103	3,780	4,130	4,983	5,700
Religion or belief	486	648	709	832	1,000
Total	23,819	39,556	41,110	35,431	38,310

Section 77 of the Equality Act makes any term of a contract void which prevents a worker from discussing pay. In the press discussion, this reform was portrayed as a key step forward, especially for those sectors such as banking and finance where such clauses have been commonplace.[35] But there are already sectors where employees have relatively high knowledge of their organisation's pay structure (the stronger the trade union organisation, the better the chance that there will be open discussions of pay, including sex discrimination in pay), and even in sectors where pay differentials are known and discussed, wide differentials persist.

THE STEFAN CROSS PHENOMENON

The use of collective equal pay claims was pioneered by a small number of solicitors, based in north-east England, who could see that sectors of the economy such as health and local government were characterised by low pay, extensive female employment and single pay scales, making them ripe for equal pay claims. The law firms have presented themselves naturally as the champions of low-paid female workers. If he has prospered, argues the best-known no-win no-fee solicitor Stefan Cross, then we should blame the employers, the trade unions and the equality organisations, none of which has done enough to challenge unequal pay:

> The highest local government manual worker grade is MWG5, or spine column point (SCP) 8. This is the grade for cooks-in-charge and home helps and they get paid £12,380 a year, or £6.41 an hour. In 1988 all manual worker posts were subject to a national job evaluation study and those jobs were rated as equivalent to refuse drivers. Yet in every single local authority the refuse drivers get paid more than every female manual worker I have dealt with.

> In Birmingham, for example, refuse drivers are paid £25,000 a year or £13.20 a hour. An untrained grade 1 refuse worker gets £21,500 or £11.13 per hour. Even a roadsweeper, also a grade 1 worker, gets £7.71 per hour – that is £1.30 per hour more than the home help who is four grades higher. Let's not forget that Birmingham City Council is an emanation of the state, it has a highly unionised workforce, is an 'equal opportunities employer' with a number of equalities officers, and is bound by the Gender Equality Duty. Despite all of this, it is still discriminating against over 30,000 female employees, more than 32 years after the Equal Pay Act.[36]

The examples cited by Stefan Cross come from local government where a national single status deal was negotiated in 1997, which required local authorities to negotiate local single-spine pay scales by April 2007. In the health service, pay is governed by Agenda for Change, a single-scale agreement reached with the unions in December 2004. One of the advantages of single-spine agreements for equal pay lawyers is that they make it easy for a claimant to compare themselves to other employees doing work of equal value, that is, equivalent but not identical work. This evades what would otherwise be a central problem of equal pay law, the difficulty of comparing poorly paid 'female' jobs and better-paid 'male' ones.[37]

The other point to note about the examples given in Cross's piece is that they have an industrial history. One of the reasons why, for example, male roadsweepers are paid better than female home helps is that in the 1970s, the roadsweepers were able to negotiate locally agreed bonus terms for work such as outdoor or wet weather work, which were incorporated into the roadsweepers' contracts and have become part of the basic package in these posts. These bonuses were won typically in a context of local strikes, usually in the 1960s and 1970s, when the manual sections of many local authorities were better organised and more strike-prone than today.[38]

From the point of view of the health and local government sectors as a whole, it could be said that an injustice is at work. These are sectors of the economy where the gap between male and female pay is relatively low,[39] and where employers have taken the most active steps to combat pay inequality, for example, by organising equal pay audits, by establishing single-scale spines, by negotiating pay with trade unions, and by publishing the outcomes of their negotiations, so that any worker can know roughly how their pay compares to everyone else's. In the process of comparing male and female pay, the sectors have in practice drawn attention to ways in which pay inequality was tolerated in the past. Yet their reward for taking the matter seriously, and for trying to reduce pay inequalities (albeit too slowly), is that their businesses are sued by thousands of workers; while other sectors such as banking and finance, which are characterised by much higher levels of pay inequality between men and women, are left alone. Bronwyn McKenna of the public sector union UNISON observes:

> The opaque nature of private sector pay means that it will be much harder for women there to challenge unequal pay. In contrast, the transparency of public sector pay means that employers who do not act to remedy glaring pay inequalities become magnets for equal pay claims.[40]

LITIGATION VERSUS BARGAINING

Stefan Cross's public approach is to blame the employers, unions and equality organisations alike for unequal pay. Yet the recruits for his equal pay cases are by and large former union members in areas of the economy where unions are recognised and active. Inevitably, that means his sharpest criticisms are reserved for the unions. Unsurprisingly, the unions have been among his greatest critics. Cross has been dubbed 'the lawyer trade unionists love to hate'.[41] Because of his notoriety, he was named in *The Times*' 2008 list of the hundred most powerful lawyers in the United Kingdom.[42] Cross has encouraged workers covered by union agreements to sue the unions for poorly negotiated pay deals.[43] In return, some unions have funded some of Cross's clients, when they have sued him successfully for charging unreasonable fees.[44]

At the heart of the dispute between Cross and the unions are two conflicting models of how pay equality should be achieved. In the private litigation model, an individual claimant, seeing that they have been subject to unequal pay, brings a case to court, is successful, and is therefore granted the difference between what they were paid and what they should have been paid in a period of up to six years prior to bringing the claim. In the collective bargaining model, a group of employees negotiates a fair pay structure, taking into account both past and *future* pay.

The attractiveness of Cross's methods derives from the many practical obstacles to fair pay. First of all, employers do not in general implement equal pay. This is true of health and local government and of the UK economy in general. Secondly, in the sectors where Cross is most active, in so far as there is any political will to implement equal pay, this is routinely defeated by the reality of resource constraint in some of the worst-funded sectors of the economy. Of course, home helps should be paid as much as refuse drivers; but employers do not have the spare money to increase home helps' pay by (in Cross's example) 100 per cent per worker. Third, the pressure has been on unions (constrained by the anti-union laws from taking a more confrontational approach), to negotiate with managers and work with them in finding solutions to problems.[45] The risk of over-reliance on partnership with employers is that it can prevent unions from approaching pay equality with the independence and militancy that the issue requires.

Yet on close consideration, the practical problems arising from tactics of mass litigation are worse. First, litigation takes money out of the sectors concerned: in health and local government, private solicitors now have on their books literally tens of thousands of claimants, and for each claimant who is successful, the solicitor will take in legal claims usually between 10 and 40 per cent of their ultimate winnings. Bronwyn McKenna of UNISON complains that workers are being enticed away from union membership by solicitors, who are portraying litigation as a cheap solution to equal pay, while simultaneously hiding from workers the extent of the contribution they will ultimately be expected to pay towards their legal costs:

> Of particular concerns are those firms that appear to have no intention of pursuing Tribunal claims, and who ride into town only when a council announces that it is willing to make back-pay offers. Such lawyers offer basic advice to low-paid women on offers already made, which the employer will generally not vary, and cream off up to 30% of the women's settlements. They tend to focus on back pay only ... We also have concerns about the lack of regulation of costs charged. One firm based in the West Midlands was quoted in *Independent Lawyer*, 1 September 2007, as saying that the size of their percentage contingency fee depends largely on 'how much competition we face from other lawyers' ... Penalty clauses are a common feature of the agreements signed with no-win no-fee lawyers. Members advise us, and we have seen agreements stating, that if they end their retainer with a no-win no-fee solicitor they will be charged £500 for every six months during which their file has been open irrespective of the amount of work carried out.[46]

Secondly, where an employer identifies that its pay structure has discriminated, there is no obligation on the employer to respond by instituting pay equality in future either for that worker individually or for the class of workers to which she belongs. Indeed, there are practical reasons why an employer, risking a Tribunal claim, might be as well advised to do nothing and wait for the decision of the courts rather than tackle the problem head on. The point can best be seen by basing two scenarios on the example given by Cross of pay inequality in Birmingham Council:

> Scenario 1: 500 female home helps are paid £6.41 per hour, which is less than 250 male roadsweepers (paid £7.71 per hour) and 250 male refuse drivers (paid £13.20 per hour). The female home helps succeed in a class action claim comparing their pay to the pay of male refuse drivers. If the home helps succeed, the employer faces a potential pay claim of £12,481 per worker per year. Multiplied by 500 workers with a 6-year employment history, this is a potential bill of £37 million.
>
> Scenario 2: (same employer, same pay structure, but in the aftermath of Scenario 1) once the employer has agreed to pay the home helps the back pay, a group of male roadsweepers (paid £7.71 per hour) commence their own 'piggy-back' claim comparing their pay to that of the female home helps (now paid £13.20 per hour). A different Tribunal accepts their claim. The employer faces an additional claim of £10,397 per worker per year. Multiplied by 250 workers with a 6-year employment history, this is an additional potential bill of £13 million.

The employer seeking to address equal pay may feel that it is better to do nothing. If it acknowledges that home helps have been paid worse than men in the past, and increases their pay on that basis, then other groups of workers may be entitled to claim that by the same reasoning they too should have been paid more. If it pre-empts the situation in Scenario 1, it may well have to make the payment in Scenario 2 also. If it does nothing, the Tribunal 'may' find that neither set of payment is necessary.

While in practice the number of workers in any pay category is usually smaller than the numbers given in the above scenarios, and only a minority of workers have the six years' service to entitle them to the full benefit of an equal pay claim (and therefore the mathematics of the above examples are not replicated in life), they illustrate the general point that a policy of equalising pay between groups of workers is likely in itself to create new and unforeseen classes of action. The law encourages employers to respond conservatively to equal pay litigation. Pay litigation tends not to result in pay equalisation and is inferior to robust collective bargaining.

The third practical problem with the solicitors' strategy of equal pay litigation, from the point of view of underpaid women workers, is that it can discourage unions from campaigning on the issue. For example, from 2006 to 2008, a number of Stefan Cross's lay clients brought a claim against the GMB trade union, regarding the union's role in accepting a pay deal in Middlesbrough which discriminated against groups of women workers. The claim was upheld against the union.[47] In the reporting of the case, it was said that equal pay solicitors had issued no less than 7,000 live claims against the GMB and 4,000 against Unison.[48] The GMB alone was said to be facing bills in the millions.[49] Perhaps not surprisingly, the GMB and other unions then became cautious about debating equal pay at events such as union national conferences, for fear that anything they said might be used against them.[50] The anxiety was that even a relatively anodyne statement to the effect that the union would be actively campaigning against pay inequality in future could be deemed to be some sort of tacit admission that the union's previous organising around the issue had been inadequate. In this way, the strategy of mass litigation by private solicitors accentuated a real problem of union defensiveness and caution.

Concerned by the very high numbers of equal pay cases, the chief executives of first the Equality Opportunities Commission,[51] and more recently the Equality and Human Rights Commission,[52] have called for an amnesty period to allow employers to put their businesses in order before further equal pay claims could be heard. It is hard to see how such a proposal could be compatible with existing UK laws on pay equality, still less in overruling the obligations contained in the constitution of the European Union and in European Directives. Even were such a proposal practicable in law, it is hard to see how it could be justified, as an amnesty would inevitably for a time lessen the pressure on employers to implement equal pay.

The reason why there are now so many equal pay cases is that solicitors have sought to bring them, and the changing dynamic of industrial relations has made them attractive to claimants. But to see the issue in these terms is inevitably to ask also whether the adoption of a strategy of individual litigation has benefited the same low-paid women workers, in whose name the claims are brought.

The argument of this chapter has been that equal pay litigation is a weak mechanism to deliver long-term pay equality. The best solution to the problem of unequal pay would rather be a reform movement for equal pay. Such a campaign would have to start within the unions. It would have to have among its demands the call for a very different kind of pay structure. There should be a massive levelling-up of pay, simplifying pay, reducing the number of grades, and consolidating the various bonuses which give rise to equal pay claims into a much smaller number of pay bands, so that the various negotiating advantages achieved in the past by male workers would be extended to all women workers as well. In a context of pervasive public sector cuts, the money to pay for this levelling-up could only be achieved by a simultaneous levelling-down of managers' salaries, which have increased dramatically in recent years in a flawed attempt to match the private sector.

The political demand should not be for a matching of home helps' to refuse drivers' wages, necessary as that is; but for a pay formula in which no council worker (cook, roadsweeper, or other) is paid less than half the salary of the Chief Executive.

Finally, it is worth recalling that the demand for equal pay was itself the creation of active trade unions characterised by distrust for managerial authority and a willingness to take strike action. The Equal Pay Act was not introduced out of the goodness of legislators' hearts. Our equal pay laws were adopted by Parliament in double quick time in 1970, in response to strikes by women workers including, most famously, the Ford equal pay strike of 1968. The women who took part in that strike manufactured car seat-covers. They were angered that their pay was 15 per cent less than their male counterparts. Their strike lasted for three weeks. Part of its success was down to the support received from other workers, including 195 women at Ford's Halewood plant in Merseyside who were also seeking equal pay. Although the unions were male-dominated at every level to a greater extent than would be allowed by any union in Britain today; unions such as the AEF, the TGWU and the NUVB gave at least equivocal support for the strikes.[53] The irony is that even while the Ford workers' demand has come to be accepted by almost everyone in the workplace, and was in 2010 celebrated in the film *Made in Dagenham*, the weakening of union power since 1968 has diminished the one agency best-placed to make equal pay a reality.

5
Why Do So Few Race Cases Win?

One feature of Employment Tribunal litigation is the different likelihood of success, faced by different claimants, depending on the jurisdiction in which their claim is brought. Of all race cases which are heard by the Tribunal, roughly one in six succeed; in contrast to (for example) wages claims, of which broadly three-quarters are upheld. There is in fact a broader pattern, in which all strands of discrimination claim have a relatively low chance of success.

Table 5.1 Claims heard at Employment Tribunals (by jurisdiction and outcome), 2010–11[1]

	Full hearings (number)	*Successful (number)*	*Chance of success*
Unlawful deduction of wages	7,500	5,400	72%
Unfair dismissal	9,000	4,200	47%
Discrimination:			
Sex	780	290	37%
Sexual orientation	84	22	26%
Disability	830	190	23%
Age	410	90	22%
Religion or belief	147	27	18%
Race	950	150	16%

Discrimination claims in general are harder to win than, say, wages or unfair dismissal claims. In no area of discrimination law does a claimant have as good a chance as a claimant in an unlawful deduction or a 'simple' unfair dismissal case.

Some of this broad picture is unsurprising. There are lots of good reasons why in general it might be easier to win deduction of wages than discrimination claims. Wages claims are simpler. They are very often undefended. Both sides usually agree that a worker was eligible to bring a claim, and therefore a typical contested wages claim might turn on an argument like a defence that the worker failed to submit accurate time sheets, or a defence that a manager had purported to give a worker a pay rise but exceeded his or her authority in so doing, or a defence that a worker did not do work of a particular kind or at a particular time or at a particular pay rate. Where there is a dispute, it can be heard quickly and is self-contained. Moreover, Employment Judges are comfortable in finding a wages case in a worker's favour. Their finding does little to disturb the orderly running of a business. It leaves the previous management hierarchies in place. It is far easier for a Tribunal to find that a worker was mistakenly underpaid £100, than it is to find that a worker was sexually harassed by a senior manager who remains in post, or was unfairly dismissed for a discriminatory reason and should now be reinstated.

The most interesting comparison is not between discrimination claims in general and wages claims as such, but *within* the category of discrimination cases. While it is possible to distinguish discrimination claims from other Tribunal cases, there is nothing specific to discrimination law or the running of the Tribunals to suggest that certain discrimination cases should be significantly easier to win than others, or indeed that race and religion should be at the bottom of the pile.

Even if some disparity between the success of claimants in different jurisdictions was inevitable, there is no obvious reason why race should be at the bottom. It could be said that age 'should' be the area of discrimination law in which employees have the worst odds of success. It is the most recent area of the law in which discrimination has been prohibited. Moreover, the structure of age discrimination law means that claimants bringing claims in this jurisdiction have less protection than claimants in other strands. In all other claims with the exception of age, an act of direct discrimination is unlawful and may *never* be justified.[2] In contrast to other discrimination jurisdictions, an employer applying a policy which directly discriminates on grounds of age (for example, a policy to refuse all internal training opportunities to all workers over the age of 60) may plead justification.

Applying a similar logic, disability cases can with very few exceptions only be brought by disabled persons;[3] for years, one obstacle to success in disability claims has been the willingness of Tribunals to grant employers a Pre-Hearing Review at which the respondent would argue that the claimant was not disabled. Where this preliminary argument has succeeded, the claim is struck out. It follows that after age, disability 'should' be the area of law where claimants should do worst.

Yet race cases are even less likely to succeed than either age or disability claims and have only half the chances of success of sex discrimination claims, which have been on the statute book for a similar period of time to race. There is something about race claims which holds Tribunals back, some factor separate from the formal structure of the law, which makes race cases harder to win.

ON RACIAL GROUNDS

Some of the difficulties faced by race claimants can be seen by looking carefully at the most high-profile cases. There have been two main sets of race discrimination cases recently which have gone to appeal; one in which a good result was achieved belatedly, and a second group which have set claimants back considerably.

The first group of cases concern the findings a Tribunal must make in order to find that a claim of race discrimination is proved. Sub-section 13(1) of the Equality Act 2010 defines direct discrimination in the following terms:

> A person (A) discriminates against another (B) if, because of a protected characteristic, A treats B less favourably than A treats or would treat others.

In section 1 of the Race Relations Act 1976 Act, which preceded the Equality Act, direct discrimination was defined as follows:

> (1) A person discriminates against another in any circumstances relevant for the purposes of any provision of this Act if –
>
> (a) on racial grounds he treats that other less favourably than he treats or would treat other persons.

Ordinarily, the phrase 'on racial grounds', or the new term 'because of' race , which replaces it, should be uncontroversial. In effect, it invites the Tribunal to ask very simply *why* a particular act occurred. If the Tribunal accepts that a discriminatory act happened because of race, then this part of the test is made out.

The difficulties have begun as a result of the second half of the sentence in the RRA starting 'on racial grounds'. The discriminator (normally the employer) must have treated a worker less favourably than another person (a 'comparator'). Three people are envisaged: A – the discriminator, B – the claimant, and C – the comparator. It is not directly stated but it must be assumed that B and C are required to be people of different racial backgrounds. (If they were not of different races, the comparator exercise would make no sense). Does this mean that for discrimination to happen A and B must also have different racial backgrounds? Some support for this possibility was provided by section 54(1)(a) of the Race Relations Act:

> A complaint by any person ('the complainant') that another person ('the respondent') –
>
> (a) has committed an act of discrimination against the complainant which is unlawful by virtue of Part II …
>
> may be presented to an employment tribunal.

The key term here is the word 'against' in the middle of the second paragraph. If discrimination must be directed *against* a claimant, then it is at least arguable that the respondent and the complainant must be of different races.

The first case to address this question dates back to the summer of 1977, when a Miss Zarczynska started work as a barmaid at a public house. The licensee and his wife did not want black people as customers and they instructed her that she should not serve them. Miss Zarczynska refused and was dismissed. The EAT had no difficulty reaching the decision that this was discriminatory treatment although both the licensee and Miss Zarczynska were white and no comparator was identified.[4]

The second case arose in April 1981, when a Mr Owens was dismissed from his post as the operator of an amusement centre for serving young black clients, who were banned as a group by his employer (a company named Showboat). Mr Owens was white. He was successful at his first hearing before the Tribunal and on appeal. The Employment Appeal Tribunal dealt with the matters of law by finding that the words 'on racial grounds' were perfectly capable of covering 'any reason for an action based on race, whether it be the race of the person affected by the action or of others'. As for the requirement of a comparator, the appropriate comparison was with another manager who had accepted the original racist instruction.[5]

Up to this point, it might appear that Tribunals had taken a sensible approach to the statute, consistent with its general purpose. In 2005, however, a third case threatened to wreck the entire apparatus of anti-discrimination law. Mr Redfearn, a member of the British National Party, worked as a bus driver. The trade union UNISON wrote to Serco complaining about Redfearn's employment. The company dismissed him, ostensibly on grounds of health and safety. Redfearn then brought a claim against the company of unlawful direct discrimination (he had not been employed continuously for a year, and could not bring the more obvious claim of ordinary unfair dismissal). Redfearn was unsuccessful at the Employment Tribunal. However, he then appealed and the Employment Appeal Tribunal ruled in Redfearn's favour, insisting that he was protected by the *Showboat* line of cases. The phrase 'on racial grounds' covered any detriment suffered by a worker, it suggested, where race was in any way a factor at all. So, for example, if a foreman treated black and white employees differently, and acted in a discriminatory fashion, and was disciplined for doing so, that foreman would be protected by the Act:

> ... although questions of motive may arise in looking at the facts as to whether there has been unfavourable treatment on racial grounds, if in fact there has been unfavourable treatment on racial grounds the goodness or badness of the relevant motive is entirely irrelevant.'[6]

At the Court of Appeal, the decision of the EAT was heavily criticised. The decision, it was said, was wrong in principle and inconsistent with the purposes of the legislation. Taken to its logical conclusion this

> ... interpretation of the 1976 Act would mean that it could be an act of direct race discrimination for an employer, who was trying to improve race relations in the workplace, to dismiss an employee, whom he discovered had committed an act of race discrimination, such as racist abuse, against a fellow employee or against a customer of the employer ... That is not the kind of case for which the anti-discrimination legislation was designed.[7]

The oddest thing about the case is that between July 2005 (the EAT decision) and May 2006 (when the case came before the Court of Appeal), as a result of Redfearn's success at the EAT, the law *was* that an employee who harassed a colleague on grounds of race was as well protected as his victim. Where cases came to the Tribunal in this time, the Tribunal was required to follow the EAT's lead.

FAILURE OF REVERSE BURDEN OF PROOF

The second group of cases concern the standard of proof that is required before a Tribunal will accept that a discrimination case is proved. The stigma associated with discrimination is greater than any other area of employment law. In direct discrimination cases in particular, the respondent is extremely unlikely to admit that they intended to treat the claimant differently. It follows that in order for claimants to have any chance of success, the Tribunal must require less evidence of a discrimination case than they would of a wages or dismissal case, but not so little that injustice is done in the opposite direction and findings of fault are made where there has in fact been no discrimination. Three decades ago, the employment courts determined that the best practical way of doing this would be to require a claimant to prove a prima facie case (that is, to put enough facts before the Tribunal to show that there was a real possibility that the behaviour had been done because of race, or sex, or any other ground). Once the Tribunal accepted that this had been done, the Tribunal could draw an inference (effectively, a provisional conclusion) that discrimination had occurred. This procedure was set out by Justice Browne-Wilkinson in the early case of *Chattopadhyay* v *Headmaster of Holloway School*:

> As has been pointed out many times, a person complaining that he has been unlawfully discriminated against faces great difficulties. There is normally not available to him any evidence of overtly racial discriminatory words or actions used by the respondent. All that the applicant can do is to point to certain facts which, if unexplained, are consistent with his having been treated less favourably than others on racial grounds. In the majority of cases it is only the respondents and their witnesses who are able to say whether in fact the allegedly discriminatory act was motivated by racial discrimination or by other, perfectly innocent, motivations. It is for this reason that the law has been established that if an applicant shows that he has been treated less favourably than others in circumstances which are consistent with that treatment being based on racial grounds, the Industrial Tribunal should draw an inference that such treatment was on racial grounds, unless the respondent can satisfy the [Tribunal] that there is an innocent explanation.[8]

By the early 1990s, higher courts in England and Wales accepted the general principle that where unlawful discrimination was a possible conclusion, the Tribunal should look to the employer for an explanation, and where there was no explanation or the explanation was inadequate, the case could or should be treated as made.[9]

Then in 2000, a European Directive was enacted requiring member states to apply a reverse burden of proof to discrimination claims.[10] The current rules are set out in section 136 of the Equality Act:

> (1) This section applies to any proceedings relating to a contravention of this Act.
> (2) If there are facts from which the court could decide, in the absence of any other explanation, that a person (A) contravened the provision concerned, the court must hold that the contravention occurred.
> (3) But subsection (2) does not apply if A shows that A did not contravene the provision.

The new idea of a reverse burden of proof was intended to be more than a mere inference. The older inference was intended to be drawn really in cases where the employer had no explanation or the explanation was clearly inadequate. The reverse burden of proof was intended to apply in a broader set of circumstances where both the claimant and the respondent had arguable cases. If the claimant had a likely case (that is, one which 'could' succeed), then the burden was on the respondent to prove it was wrong. This should involve more than a merely adequate defence.

In a criminal case before the Crown Court, the jurors are told not to convict unless they are 'sure' of a defendant's guilt. In the older terminology, which is rarely used in the courts today (but still appears in courtroom dramas), the same standard was described as 'beyond reasonable doubt'. The older phrase is useful because it reminds us that a juror can convict where they have a minimum residual doubt. The mere fact that a defendant has insisted on pleading not guilty suggests that some facts must weigh in her favour. But if the vast majority of the key facts point towards guilt, with the result that the jurors are sure, then they should convict.

In civil cases, including employment cases, and no matter the seriousness of the allegation,[11] there is only one standard of proof: 'on the balance of probabilities'. The standard is much lower than in criminal cases. A trial judge in the High Court can find that a particular event occurred even if the judge is not sure that it did. But there is still a slightly higher burden on the person bringing the case than there is on the person defending it. If the case is finely balanced, it should usually be decided in favour of whichever side has the slight advantage. But if the case is exactly balanced, then the decision should be against the person bringing the claim, because in the last resort it is their case, they have brought it, and it is right therefore to place the burden on them to persuade the court that their case is true. The test is never put like this, but in practice a judge should find for the claiming party where that party has persuaded them that it is 51 per cent likely that the event occurred.

Reverse burdens of proofs are not unique to employment, and can be found elsewhere in the law.[12] The general idea of a reverse burden in civil cases is that where a claimant shows there is a possible or good case to answer (say, that their case has a 25 per cent chance of success), the burden moves to the other party. There is still ultimately a 51 per cent hurdle, but now it rests against the defending party to refute the claim. This is the principle of a reverse burden; there is nothing in the Race Relations Act to suggest that anything more complex than this was intended.

In 2006, the Court of Appeal heard three cases all of which concerned this statutory provision. The first case, *Brown* v *Croydon London Borough Council*, concerned a black employee of Croydon Council who was told by his white male manager that female colleagues found him threatening. The black worker told his manager that if this was true their complaints should be investigated. The manager declined to do so. The manager did, however, extend the claimant's probationary period to 18 months into his employment. The manager falsely accused the claimant of working on his own account running a child-minding business during working hours and of dishonesty in his travelling expenses. The Tribunal simply disregarded the first step of the burden of proof, saying that if there was evidence of misconduct by the white manager, there was no evidence of racism. When the case came to the Court of Appeal, this approach was endorsed by the Court.

There are two points to make in commenting on this case. First, *Brown* could easily have been decided differently. Clearly, the white manager had treated the claimant badly. Moreover, in at least one of the ways he did so, by suggesting that the black employee was behaving threateningly to white women, he was within the terrain of racist stereotyping. Secondly, there is no reason of principle why it should disfavour a black claimant to say that Tribunals can skip the first stage of the reverse burden of proof. There is no problem *so long as the ultimate requirement is still on the employer to disprove the case*. Up to now, the Court was reading statute at face value. Up to this point, the law was not being made more difficult for other claimants.

The second case, *Appiah & Anor* v *Bishop Douglas Roman Catholic High School*, was not an employment matter but an education case. It is relevant to employment law, however, because the same principle (that is, the operation of the reversed burden) was at stake. Four students were involved in a fight at a school, two of whom were black and two white. The two black students were excluded; the two white students were not. The case was initially heard at the High Court, where the boys provided a great deal of evidence to suggest that their exclusion had been racially motivated. One of their parents gave evidence of institutional discrimination at the school. Figures were provided showing that there were a very high level of exclusions, and that many more black than white students were excluded. Evidence was provided to show that the school authorities investigating the two black boys had used loaded language against them in the investigation – for example, describing them as 'animals'. The investigator had failed to complete his investigation within the statutory time limits (with the result that the black students had been kept on an indefinite informal suspension). The investigator was generous with his time to the parents of the white students, and rude to the parents of the black students. The black students had served a statutory questionnaire and the school's answers to it had been evasive. The High Court upheld the exclusions, as did the Court of Appeal. The leading speech was given by Lord Justice Maurice Kay, who said:

> In the present case, as in any other, the mere establishment of a difference of race and a difference in treatment is not enough to cause the burden to be transferred under section 57ZA. It is for the claimant at least to establish facts from which it could be inferred that there has been discrimination 'on racial grounds' … If, having considered *all* the evidence, the court or tribunal comes to the conclusion that the facts do not establish a prima facie case of a difference in treatment on racial grounds, no burden is transferred.[13]

The key sentence is the last one. Here, for the first time, the Court of Appeal was subtly altering the reverse burden of proof. What it was suggesting was that in order for a claimant to satisfy the first step of the reversal of the burden, the claimant needed to do enough to convince a Tribunal that their case was made out. In deciding this, both the claimant's evidence and the respondent's evidence were relevant. It was not enough, for example, for the claimants to show (as they had here) that two black students had been treated one way and two white students had been treated very much better. The claimants did not do enough to prove an initial case. *Something more was needed*, although quite what was not spelled out.

The third case, *Madarassy* v *Nomura International plc*, concerned a pregnant employee who was dismissed and brought claims of sex discrimination.[14] Ms Madarassay's case had been heard by the Tribunal over 21 days, with 32 witnesses. The Tribunal analysed the burden of proof as follows:

> We have then considered whether Ms Madarassy was treated any less favourably than a hypothetical male comparator would have been treated in the same circumstances and, if so, whether it was on the grounds of her sex or pregnancy. If so, the Tribunal has to consider whether the Respondent has proved that it did not commit the act in question.

Ms Madarassy appealed from the Tribunal and much of her attack was aimed at this direction. The Court analysed the reversal of the burden of proof in exhaustive terms and this is now the leading case on the matter. Essentially, Ms Madarassay's complaint was that the Tribunal had failed to apply the correct test, depriving her of the benefit of the reversal of the burden of proof. The Tribunal had scrutinised her case and rejected it. It should have scrutinised Nomura's case and rejected the adequacy of Nomura's explanation for its discriminatory treatment of her.

Lord Justice Mummery's judgment was wholly against Ms Madarassy. On a proper interpretation of the reverse burden of proof, he found, a Tribunal should go through a two-step procedure. First, the Tribunal should ask whether there is a prima facie case of discrimination. In seeing if this standard is met, Mummery (repeating the Court in *Appiah*) found that the evidence of both the respondent and the claimant should be considered. Only if there was a prime facie case would the burden shift to the employer.[15] Although Mummery was nowhere precise on how high the claimant's initial burden stands, in general terms, it is not less than the balance of probabilities.

The decision in *Madarassay* was in effect that for a Tribunal to accept that a case is made out, the claimant has to persuade it (to the 51 per cent standard) that the respondent has a case to answer. To do this, it must persuade the Tribunal that its entire case is well-founded. That point being accepted, the employer still has the chance to refute the case (with the 51 per cent standard now applying to them).

The whole merit of the revered burden of proof was that in order to engage it, the Claimant only had to have a likely prime facie case (in the language of the Equality Act, there have to be facts from which the Tribunal 'could' infer discrimination) and, since the decision in *Madarassy*, the majority of Tribunals have acted as if the statutory obligation was only engaged in the most unusual of cases. The ordinary jurisprudence of the Employment Tribunal is now very little different from what it would be if the reversed burden had never applied. There are, moreover, dynamics specific to race claims which mean that the failure to implement the reversed burden as the legislation was original intended will fall especially hard on race claimants, in contrast to claimants in other areas of discrimination law.

THE INTRUSION OF NON-LEGAL REASONING

When speaking to non-lawyers about discrimination law, they will often make guesses about what the law says. Their guesses reflect the common-sense values of society as a whole. So, for example, it is often assumed that racism is a particularly onerous charge to be levied against any individual. An individual, it follows, should only be found to have done an act of race discrimination if they clearly intended to discriminate. Moreover, it is assumed that any person associated with an act of race discrimination must be 'a racist'. This rule of common-sense understanding is best applied in reverse: where an individual does not display clear and evident signs of 'racism' in all their ordinary day-to-day behaviour, then by definition they are incapable of having committed an act of discrimination.

Yet the law contains no test of intention. In the majority of cases, a claimant brings a claim of discrimination against the employer. The employer is deemed liable for the acts of his employees even where those acts were done without his knowledge or approval. The issue before the Tribunal is the conduct, not the person.

It is clear from early cases such as *Chattopadhyay* that the reason the courts moved away from 'common-sense' ways of thinking about race discrimination is because (where they are followed) they are singularly unlikely to result in any findings of race discrimination at all. If we consider the sort of factual nexus that was found in *Showboat* (that is, an instruction to discriminate); if a black customer had brought a claim to the county courts complaining of discrimination in the provision of goods and services, the company could easily have defended itself by saying that there was in fact no rule that its employees should discriminate. We know that there was a rule, and we know that because of the bravery of the claimant Mr Owens, but without him the discrimination would not have become known, and in the majority of employment cases, there is no one who plays such a part. A manager discriminates against an employee and in doing so the manager probably has no more fully formed thought than that he dislikes his black employee. The manager will not discuss his likes or dislikes with anyone else. If there is anyone to whom the manager speaks, that person is unlikely to break ranks afterwards because they too will fear dismissal. No one challenges the behaviour. As a result, black employees are on average worse paid than white employees,[16] more likely to be dismissed by their employer, and take longer to move from periods of unemployment to employment.[17] There are real phenomena of scapegoating and stereotyping; the concept of institutional racism explains genuine trends in our society.

Seen from the perspective of challenging racism, the whole history of the Tribunals is a story of real attempts to confront racism followed by retreats. In 1997 and 1998, the Tribunal heard the case of Dr Anya, who had been unsuccessful in an application for a post as Postdoctoral Research Assistant in Materials at Oxford University. Two applicants had been considered for the position, one black, one white, and the white candidate had been accepted. Dr Anya complained that the application process had been stacked against him from the outset. The panel making the appointment contained a Dr Roberts, who had been Dr Anya's supervisor over the previous two years (during which time Dr Anya had been employed on a similar research assistantship in the same department). Dr Anya complained that Dr Roberts had been uncooperative with him through this time; had told him before the post was advertised 'you can apply if you want, but you will not get it'; that shortly before the interview, the job description was changed so as to reduce the obstacles facing the white candidate who would not otherwise have had enough experience to be appointed; and that after the interview, the university attempted to cover up the reasons for its decision. The Tribunal heard the case over eleven days, and by the language of its own judgment appears to have had real difficulty in choosing between the conflicting evidence of Dr Roberts and Dr Anya. The Tribunal failed to say whether any of Dr Anya's specific complaints were made out, but on what it considered was the central question (had Dr Roberts' treatment of the claimant been motivated by racism?), it decided that the conduct was not discriminatory:

> It would be inappropriate for us to characterise any of the witnesses coming before us in this hearing as being untruthful, but we have to say that we regard Dr Roberts and Professor Cantor as being essentially witnesses of truth despite the inconsistencies that were exposed under skilful cross-examination.
>
> The unanimous view of the Tribunal is that we are satisfied that the applicant received less favourable treatment in that Dr Lawrence was appointed when he was not. We are invited to draw the inference that was because of his race and not, as the respondents claim, on a genuine assessment of his scientific strengths and weaknesses. We are disposed to accept the respondents' explanation and in our view the evidence is not sufficient to justify us in drawing the inference of discrimination.

Whatever other criticisms could be made of this decision, what is most interesting is that the Tribunal reverted to a common-sense analysis of racism. Dr Roberts had told the truth and therefore he could not be a bad person. If he was a good person, his conduct could not have amounted to race discrimination.

On Dr Anya's appeal to the EAT, the judgment was endorsed. It was possible, the Tribunal held, that Dr Anya's skills had not properly been fostered in the department, but 'improbable'. It was possible that the selection process for the relevant job had been discriminatory but 'plainly improbable'. It was possible that the department had closed ranks against Dr Anya, but again 'improbable'. The EAT concluded in terms which were critical of Dr Anya for persisting with what the Appeal Tribunal evidently decided was a hopeless case: 'Nobody in the context of a complaint of racial discrimination could have listened to evidence over so many days without a growing and legitimate realisation that Dr Anya's task of proving such [discrimination] was speculative to the point of being hopeless.'[18]

The EAT had no particular reason for suggesting that it was improbable that Dr Roberts had mistreated Dr Anya, or had treated him with hostility when assessing his skills for the post, or had encouraged colleagues to reject Dr Anya's complaints, because the Tribunal had made no rulings that these allegations were true or untrue. If anything, of course, the Tribunal had found that differential treatment *did* occur, just that Dr Roberts had been telling the truth when he said that the reason for the differential treatment was not race. Nothing appears to have justified the EAT's remarks that Dr Anya's case was improbable other than a belief that any claim of race discrimination is by its nature, unlikely to be true.

At the Court of Appeal, the Tribunal's decision was overturned and the case was remitted to a new Tribunal. Lord Justice Sedley held that 'Experience of other cases indicates, speaking generally, that the allegations made by Dr Anya are not inherently improbable; nor, if his factual allegations are made out, are the reasons for them necessarily speculative.' The problem with the Tribunal's conclusions of facts is that it had so focused on the question of whether Dr Roberts had been motivated by racism, that it had failed to consider the smaller factual issues which should have determined whether such a complaint was properly made out or not. The Tribunal had been wrong to fix narrowly on the question of whether Dr Roberts had been truthful. It should have asked rather whether there was evidence that he treated black employees differently in comparison to white employees, or not.[19]

Coming back from *Anya* to *Redfearn* v *Serco,* we can see that the determination with which the EAT held to its interpretation of the *Showboat* line of authorities (flawed and contrary to principle as it must now appear), was not some aberration in the history of the Employment Tribunals, but part of a long story of haphazard and unpredictable judgments, arising from ultimately irreconcilable tendencies within both legal and especially non-legal thinking about race.

The point has already been made that although *Madarassy* was a sex discrimination case, the narrowing of the reversal of the burden of proof by that case is likely to fall hardest on race claimants. It is noticeable that, with the exception of *Madarassy* itself, the large majority of the reported cases on the reverse burden of proof have been race claims.[20] Race claimants emphasise this part of the law more in their pleadings and in practice rely more on it. They depend on it more because race claimants face a greater credibility hurdle than claimants in sex and disability discrimination cases. In all three strands of the law, the judges do their best to implement the rules that make discrimination unlawful. But the practical consequence of their decisions is that countless race claimants in particular are simply disbelieved. This raises the question of why they are disbelieved.

ORAL EVIDENCE IN RACE CASES

Race discrimination was described 25 years ago by Lord Justice Mummery as 'the most difficult kind of case' that the Tribunals must decide:

> The legal and evidential difficulties are increased by the emotional content of the cases. Feelings run high. The complainant alleges that he has been unfairly and unlawfully treated in an important respect affecting his employment, his livelihood, his integrity as a person. The person against whom an accusation of discrimination is made feels that his acts and decisions have been misunderstood, that he has been unfairly, even falsely, accused of serious wrongdoing.[21]

Race cases tend, more than other claims, to pit the evidence of two people directly against one another. Arguably, this is a situation in which the Tribunal should flourish. While an Employment Judge may be new in post or unfamiliar with a particular line of authorities, it is of the essence of the Tribunals that the Judges are experts at choosing between conflicting witnesses.

By no means do all legal systems put such an emphasis on the importance of oral testimony.[22] But in common law courts, the situation is constantly repeated: a witness gives evidence, a lawyer asks questions, some sort of adjudicator decides.

Part of the problem lies in this very relationship between judge and witness. The latter has too much invested in the relationship; the former (like a millionaire donor suffering from 'compassion fatigue') is over-conditioned to disbelief.

Thinking away from employment law for a moment; in a recent study of the UK immigration courts, the anthropologist Anthony Good was struck by the contrast between the way in which people applying for asylum and lawyers or judges thought about the process of giving evidence. For the applicant, what matters most is their evidence in chief (that is, when they give their evidence, initially, in the form of a speech). This is their chance to tell their story. What matters to the lawyers however is the cross-examination (that is, when the applicant is asked questions) and in particular the extent to which the witness comes over as credible or not when questioned. For a presenting officer of the Home Office (the nearest equivalent to a respondent's representative in the Employment Tribunal), the key task is to establish small inconsistencies between the different accounts given by asylum applicants. If these add up, a legal submission can be made that the applicant's account lacks credibility. For the applicant's representative, the best that can be hoped is that their client comes out with their story as little tarnished as possible. Good went on to give various reasons for why applicant testimony tended to be disbelieved by asylum courts. He described the operation of various common-sense assumptions about the ways in which people gave evidence. For example:

> Common sense teaches that people tell their whole story at every opportunity;
> Common sense teaches that traumatic events will be recalled vividly;
> Common sense teaches that stories will be told in a logical narrative.[23]

As an anthropologist, with many years' experience of listening to people telling their life stories, Good suggested that all of these assumptions were false. It is perfectly natural that a person would only divulge a full narrative of a painful incident only over time, whether from feelings of shame, or because of a lack of trust in the first authority to which they were supposed to tell the full story. In general, traumatic incidents are often badly recalled. Certain kinds of pain resist language or even destroy it. The more intense the suffering that a person has gone through, the worse they will be at talking about it afterwards. When a person seeks to recall unpleasant events, their memory of them is often non-linear; an inability to recall them in a chronological narrative is no better a sign of dishonesty than of real pain.

Watching the asylum courts at close hand, Good was struck by the willingness of adjudicators to make credibility rulings on the basis of such false reasoning. He described 'avoidance reactions' where adjudicators would deal with the emotional distress of unpleasant evidence by showing a profound lack of empathy with those giving evidence. He identified what he thought was an over-reliance on demeanour by adjudicators in deciding whether or not to believe particular witnesses. He cited one unpublished survey of asylum adjudicators, conducted by a part-time adjudicator, in which fellow adjudicators were asked to explain why they believed one witness and disbelieved another: 'Replies indicated considerable variation in stated practice and showed that many credibility decisions rested on adjudicators' "gut feelings", their application of common sense (possibly another way of saying the same thing), or recourse to personal experience.'[24]

A typical race case is in some ways like and in other ways unlike a typical asylum case. The emotional intensity of the experiences narrated by the employment claimant will be in all likelihood far less (many asylum cases turn after all on accounts of rape, torture, or being made to watch killings). Yet many race cases have something like the same dynamic. Like asylum applicants, race claimants see themselves as telling a story of truth to power. Like asylum applicants, the essence of race claimants' narratives is a story of suffering. People bring to the Tribunal stories about being bullied, being called names, sometimes about being threatened or physically attacked, and almost always about the failure of their employers to investigate their serious complaints. Very often a race claimant will break down in tears.

The Judges who hear asylum cases and employment cases are very similar people.[25] They have the same formal training. They are the products of the same common law legal culture, with the same emphasis on credibility, and the same tendency to look for 'common-sense' markers that a particular witness is or is not telling the truth. There are dynamics in asylum cases which encourage a culture of disbelief in the courts. The same institutional pressures to disbelief can be found in race claims before the Employment Tribunal.

6 Human Rights Decisions in the Tribunal

I'm an Employment Lawyer, What has the Human Rights Act done for me? Not much, yet.[1]

Moral righteousness is insufficient to win a legal point in the courtroom.[2]

Over the past ten years, the Tribunal has seen a concerted attempt by several lawyers, often claimant representatives, to develop a culture of human rights-sensitive decision making. In assessing the extent to which this attempt has succeeded, it is important to have a realistic measure of success. Human rights have been directly enforceable in the UK only since 2 October 2000, when the Human Rights Act 1998 ('HRA') came into effect. Section 2 of the Act provides that 'A court or tribunal determining a question which has arisen in connection with a Convention right must take into account any judgment, decision, declaration or advisory opinion of the European Court of Human Rights ... .' Section 3 of the Act provides 'So far as it is possible, primary and subordinate legislation must be read and given effect in a way which is compatible with the Convention rights ... .' Convention rights are rights under the European Convention of Human Rights, as listed in Table 6.1.

The significance of section 3 of the HRA is that 'legislation' means *all* legislation, in whatever area. Precisely because Convention rights are very widely drawn, it is hard to think of any area of law where the HRA has made no difference, and there has not been at least some attempt to use the Act to have legislation read dynamically. That said, it is equally clear that in no area of law has the HRA completely reversed all that was previously fixed. The European Convention was drafted at the end of the Second World War, very largely by British lawyers infused with a sense of the virtues of the common law tradition, and seeking to impose its habits in place of the old legal systems of the former fascist states.[3] The return to the UK of familiar concepts, albeit with new labels, was never likely to revolutionise our law. Moreover, the interpretation of the HRA

Table 6.1 Principal rights listed under the European Convention of Human Rights[4]

Article 2	Right to life
Article 3	Prohibition of torture
Article 4	Prohibition of slavery and forced labour
Article 5	Right to liberty and security
Article 6	Right to a fair trial
Article 7	No punishment without law
Article 8	Right to respect for private and family life
Article 9	Freedom of thought, conscience, religion
Article 10	Freedom of expression
Article 11	Freedom of assembly and association
Article 12	Right to marry
Article 14	Prohibition of discrimination
Protocol 1, Article 1	Protection of property
Protocol 1, Article 2	Right to education
Protocol 1, Article 3	Right to free elections
Protocol 6, Article 1	Abolition of death penalty

has been left to a cadre of judges who whether out of timidity or from a realistic sense of the unattractiveness of judicial intervention overturning laws made by democratic parliaments, have tried to avoid ushering in a new era of judicial creativity. The HRA was never going to change all employment law, neither was it going to leave everything exactly as it was before.

Compared to other areas of law, how far has employment law changed? In several legal fields, the HRA has been used to great effect. Two examples will suffice. The first is the law regarding the detention of terrorist suspects. In *A and others* v *Secretary of State for the Home Department*,[5] the House of Lords had to consider whether the indefinite detention of foreign nationals in Belmarsh Prison without trial under section 23 of the Anti-terrorism, Crime and Security Act 2001 was compatible with the European Convention of Human Rights and, in particular, in so far as the 2001 Act purported to disapply article 5 of the Convention which prohibits arbitrary detention, whether this derogation was lawful (it could only be lawful if the threat of terrorism was a public emergency threatening the life of the nation). The House of Lords found that there was an emergency, but that the measures chosen to protect the public were unnecessary and therefore that section 23 was unlawful.

The second example is housing law. The 2010 case *Manchester* v *Pinnock*,[6] asked whether a court, making an order for possession against a tenant, was required to give the tenant an opportunity of a public hearing, in which they could set out certain basic circumstances about themselves and say why the order should not be made. This question had particular force because successive Acts of Parliament have set out a range of circumstances in which a tenant has diminished security of tenure and no right to such a hearing: for example, where a tenant has already been found to have committed acts of anti-social behaviour and a 'demotion order' has been made against them, or where a tenant has been granted their tenancy under local authority powers intended to enable the rapid (and therefore impermanent) housing of former homeless persons. *Manchester* v *Pinnock* is of particular interest to employment lawyers, not just because of the content of the final decision (which was that as a consequence of article 8 of the Convention tenants do have a right to such a hearing), but because of the complicated pre-history of the litigation, which involved the House of Lords finding in no fewer than three high-profile cases[7] that there was no such right, being overruled in full once[8] and once in part[9] by the European Court of Human Rights at Strasbourg. When the Judges of the Supreme Court revisited these decisions in 2010, they had to find that they themselves had repeatedly been wrong. A liberalisation of the law was achieved by a small number of lawyers committed to human rights fighting test cases with focused concentration over a period of ten years. Their victory shows that the Human Rights Act widens the scope of the decisions that the courts themselves are willing to make.

From the list of rights in the European Convention, which was set out earlier in this chapter, it will be clear that the Convention is at least potentially capable of having a similar liberalising effect on employment law. Just to take a few examples, Article 8 of the European Convention provides that:

1. Everyone has the right to respect for his private and family life, his home and his correspondence.
2. There shall be no interference by a public authority with the exercise of this right except such as is in accordance with the law and is necessary in a democratic society in the interests of national security, public safety or the economic well-being of the country, for the prevention of disorder or crime, for the protection of health or morals, or for the protection of the rights and freedoms of others.

In non-employment litigation, the right to private life has found to comprise a right not to be spied upon,[10] not to have property removed,[11] and not to have private activities reported in a public forum,[12] save according to the limited exceptions in article 8(2).

Again, article 11 of the European Convention provides that:

1. Everyone has the right to freedom of peaceful assembly and to freedom of association with others, including the right to form and to join trade unions for the protection of his interests.[13]

On the face of it, this should protect workers who join or are active in unions, as well as others criticised by their employers for their associations inside or outside of work. Meanwhile, other rights protected in the Convention include the right to a fair hearing (article 6 – this is relevant to grievance and disciplinary hearings in the workplace), the right not to suffer discrimination (article 14), and the right to practice a profession (which is covered by article 1 of the First Protocol to the Convention).[14]

Although few employment cases have been heard by the European Court of Human Rights, those cases which have been heard have taken a purposive attitude towards workers' rights. In 1997, the ECHR determined the case of *Halford* v *United Kingdom*, concerning a police officer whose phone was tapped at work in order to assist the Merseyside force in defending a sex discrimination claim. The Court held:

> There is no evidence of any warning having been given to Ms Halford, as a user of the internal telecommunications system operated at the Merseyside police headquarters, that calls made on that system would be liable to interception. She would, the Court considers have had a reasonable expectation of privacy for such calls … .[15]

The 2007 case of *Copland* v *United Kingdom*[16] considered a worker in a further education college whose e-mails, telephone calls and internet usage was monitored by her employer. This conduct was found to breach article 8 of the Convention.[17]

In *Wilson and Palmer* v *United Kingdom*,[18] two litigants complained that their employer had paid bonuses to reward only those of its employees who would agree not join a union. The ECHR emphasised the importance of the right to join a union and the practical implications that follow from that right:

> It is of the essence of the right to join a trade union for the protection of their interests that employees should be free to instruct or permit the union to make representations to their employer or to take action in support of their interests on their behalf. If workers are prevented from so doing, their freedom to belong to a trade union, for the protection of their interests, becomes illusory. It is the role of the State to ensure that trade union members are not prevented or restrained from using their union to represent them in attempt to regulate their relations with employers.[19]

As we have seen, section 3 of the Human Rights Act requires any court in the UK, including the Employment Tribunal and the EAT, to read legislation compatibly with any relevant Convention rights. In cases which have considered what sort of reading is allowed, it has been said that where a right is at stake and it is inadequately protected by any Act, the reading may be a strained interpretation, or that a non-literal construction may be adopted, or that words may be read in by way of addition to those used by the legislator.[20] For common law lawyers, who are trained to read Acts of Parliament literally, squeezing every possible drop of meaning from the slightest variation in the actual words of a statute, this is a liberation indeed.

A good indication of how a purposive interpretation can work is provided by *Attridge Law* v *Coleman*, in which the EAT determined that a Tribunal was required to read the Disability Discrimination Act ('DDA') in a way so as to give effect to the European law rights of a carer for a disabled person, and this meant reading the DDA as if the Act had a series of additional sub-sections protecting not merely disabled persons but also persons associated with a disabled person. Section 3A of the DDA was to be read as if the Parliament had include the underlined words

> 3A Meaning of 'discrimination ...
> (5A) A person also directly discriminates against a person if he treats him less favourably than he treats or would treat another person <u>by reason of the disability of another person</u>.[21]

The Tribunal has the power to read legislative in a purposive fashion, testing our existing employment laws against the rights set out in the Convention. But this is to state its powers in general terms – what in practice has it done?

THE HUMAN RIGHTS ACT IN THE EMPLOYMENT COURTS

The first significant case on the application of the Human Rights Act in an employment setting was *X* v *Y*.[22] The claimant was a case worker for a charity with young offenders promoting their personal development. He was cautioned by the police after being caught having sex with another man in a toilet. He did not tell his employers about the caution, but when the information came to the knowledge of his employer he was dismissed. The case concerned the operation of section 98 of the ERA, which governs the fairness of dismissal, where the dismissal was said to have interfered with a claimant's rights under articles 8 and 14. The criticism of the dismissal was that the employee's sexual activities took place outside work and were of no concern of the employer. Investigating them breached the claimant's right to respect for private life, and in so far as unfair dismissal law allowed the employer to rely on information gathered covertly, and indeed required the Tribunal to approach the fairness of a dismissal from the effective presumption that the dismissal was fair,[23] this law was incompatible with the European Convention.

The rights set out in the Convention are rights which the state must protect in its relationship with its citizens. There had long been a controversy as to whether these were also intended to have effect in relationships between citizens, with some authorities arguing that they were not (the express language of the Convention is to place the burden on states rather than citizens),[24] and others arguing that they were. Prior to *X* v *Y*, it was genuinely unclear how far private employment relationships in the UK were subject to Convention principles. The Court of Appeal, showing its liberal face, found that the European Convention did not merely place burdens on public bodies, it also governed the relationships between private citizens: 'In private employment disputes, the employment tribunal, so far as it is possible to do so, must read and give effect to s98 and the other relevant provisions in Part X of the ERA in a way which is compatible with the Convention right in article 8 and article 14.'[25]

Yet the Court went on to find, that the claimant's article 8 rights were not protected for the reason that (in general) private sexual activities were not protected by article 8 if the activities were short-lived and if they were criminal offences:

> The sexual activity was transitory, and took place in a public lavatory between two strangers. Moreover, whatever the precise nature of the sexual activity, it was sufficient to amount to gross

> indecency. In my judgment, neither of the participants could have had a reasonable expectation of privacy in those circumstances.[26]

It is hard to find merit in the reasoning that the sexual activities of a gay man having sex with a stranger, simply because these activities are transitory, require *in principle* less protection than the sexual activities of (say) a heterosexual man who has been having sex with his wife intermittently in the same bed for 30 or more years.

The next important case on the interaction between ordinary employment legislation and the Human Rights Act was *Pay* v *Lancashire Probation Service*, a decision of the EAT,[27] which was heard subsequently by the European Court of Human Rights. The claimant was a probation officer, whose duties included the treatment of sex offenders. It came to his employer's attention that he was also in his evenings and at weekends a director of an organisation (Roissy) selling sex toys and organising sexual events connected with bondage, domination and sadomasochism. The employer investigated his activities, obtaining photographs of the claimant and others, semi-naked, performing sexual acts which had taken place at a local private member's club. The claimant was dismissed.

In a pattern not dissimilar to that seen in *X* v *Y*, the EAT in *Pay* was willing to grant a considerable part of the claimant's legal argument, while determining the case against him on its facts. The Employment Appeal Tribunal accepted that section 3 of the HRA has an impact on unfair dismissal law.[28] It went on to find however that article 8 had not been engaged, and the employer's investigation of the claimant's sexual activities breached no privacy right.

The Court of Human Rights found that the applicant's activities took place in a nightclub frequented by a self-selecting group of like-minded individuals. Photos of the applicant appeared on the Roissy website but with his features concealed. In contrast to the Court of Appeal in *X* v *Y*, the Court of Human Rights found that Mr Pay's sexual activities were private and he was entitled to protection. The Court went on to find however that in general terms an employee owes his employer a duty of loyalty, reserve and discretion. Mr Pay's job involved working closely with convicted sex offenders who had been released from prison. It was incumbent on him to maintain the respect of the offenders placed under his supervision and also the confidence of the public including victims of sex crime. In so far as the dismissal had interfered with the claimant's rights under article 8, this interference was justified.[29]

Both *X* and *Pay* concerned the right to privacy of people perceived by the courts as sexual minorities. To make matters still more difficult, the claimants' strategies to win their cases required the courts to agree to overturn the conventional interpretation of unfair dismissal law, which has been subject to litigation over many years, and is understood by the courts in a manner intended to represent a crafted balance between the interests of employers and workers. This was too much to ask.

The next significant case on the interpretation of the Convention was *Copsey* v *Devon Clays*,[30] which concerned a claimant who might perhaps be expected to find it easier to gain the ear of the Tribunal. The claimant was a machine operator and a Christian who was opposed in principle to Sunday working. In the Court of Appeal, Mummery LJ insisted that the case involved balancing competing rights of large numbers of people and as such was inherently unsuitable for litigation:

> Courts do not have access to the same range of expertise or to the same consultative procedures as legislation. Neither judges nor lawyers have relevant knowledge or experience. The adversarial trial processes in the courts and tribunals are not suited to deciding questions of this kind.[31]

As for the point of principle, whenever similar cases had come before the European Court of Human Rights they had been decided in favour of the employer. The right to have a religion is protected by article 9. But it was only protected to a limited extent. In so far as a worker's religion requires him to leave his employment, or causes his employer to dismiss him directly, such treatment is deemed insufficient to be an infringement of the Convention right.

There was for a time a modest incremental development of human rights practice in the employment field, in the relatively narrow area of professional conduct proceedings. These proceedings may concern, say, a nurse, or teacher, or doctor, and will determine that professional's fitness to practice their profession, not just with her present employer but at all. Usually, there will be an investigation in the workplace before fitness to practice proceedings. In some cases, both sets of proceedings are accompanied by criminal proceedings. The Court of Appeal held in *R (on the application of G)* v *X School Governors* that where fitness to practice proceedings are likely, a professional is entitled to a very high level of procedural fairness in the original workplace investigation, which may extend, for example, to a right to be represented by a solicitor in a misconduct hearing; although this decision was ultimately overturned by the Supreme Court.[32]

More typical of the handling of human rights claims before the Tribunal is the case of *Dooley* v *Balfour Beatty Ltd*, which was heard at the Employment Tribunal in London Central in 2010. The claimant, who was unrepresented, was a former building worker and latterly an official of the building workers' union UCATT. He complained that in 1993 he had been dismissed from a post with Balfour Beatty, after which he had applied again to Balfour Beatty for employment and been unsuccessful. In the early 1990s, Balfour Beatty had been a member of an organisation known as the Consulting Association, an association of construction industry employers who shared a covert database of information concerning their employees, principally trade union activists. The work of the Consulting Association seeped into the public domain and in 2009, the Information Commissioner, the body charged with enforcing the UK's data protection laws, raided the Consulting Association and released to the workers involved the files held about them. Dooley's own file included allegations that he was a member of an unofficial network of construction militants and that he had occupied a crane during a dispute over pay. The strength of Dooley's claim was that he could show that he had been subject to covert data collection. The weakness of his claim was that his allegations of unfair dismissal and refusals to appoint for reasons of trade union activities were heard 17 years after the event, Dooley's own memory of the period was vague and subject to change, and the Tribunal was far from persuaded that Balfour had ever either employed or dismissed him. In the relevant period, it found, it was more likely that he had been engaged via a third-party subcontractor. Dooley sought to overcome these difficulties by relying on a purposive interpretation of the law. The Tribunal reminded itself of the relevant law:

> The Human Rights Act 1998 offers protection for the right to respect for private and family life (Article 8) and the rights to freedom of expression (Article 10) and freedom of Association (Article 11). The right to respect for private life may be relevant in this case. Whether the contents of the blacklist originate in the public domain or not or have been obtained by any covert or intrusive method or not, the blacklist itself is a permanent record such that private life considerations arise. The Tribunal, as a public authority, is under a duty to apply the law so as to accord

> with the provisions of the Act and to interpret the law in a way which gives a result compatible with the rights arising under the Act. It does not however directly confer any new private causes of action on individuals where their rights have been violated by a private party.

The Tribunal went on to determine the case in favour of the employer:

> The basis of our decision is factual findings to the effect that Mr Dooley was not an employee of Balfour Beatty and did not after his employment was terminated approach them for employment. This is not a question of the interpretation of statutory rights or the giving effect to rights introduced by the Act: there is no free standing claim and our findings do not give rise to the application of the provisions of the Act.

In being blacklisted, Mr Dooley had undoubtedly suffered wrong. But in the context of the claim that was actually before the Tribunal, and the vagueness of the evidence given by him, the Tribunal could not be criticised for reaching this decision.

Another case, *Fosh* v *Cardiff University*,[33] concerned an academic specialising in Labour Relations and Human Resource Management. In 2003, one of Dr Fosh's former students issued a race claim against Cardiff University. Initially, his claim was backed by the Commission for Racial Equality. The Commission unfortunately withdrew and Dr Fosh took on her representation. Her employer asked her to withdraw, which she declined to do. Dr Fosh was suspended by the university, and a thorough search was conducted of her work email account, from which it was found that she had sent emails critical of her line manager to several former students. Dr Fosh was dismissed for misconduct. She brought a claim to the Employment Tribunal which was unsuccessful and then appealed. Part of her complaint concerned the employer's reliance on material gathered from the monitoring of her emails.

At the EAT, Dr Fosh's representative referred to *Copland* v *UK* (discussed earlier in this chapter) arguing that in her case, as in *Copland*, monitoring of her emails had been a breach of her rights under article 8. The EAT found against Dr Fosh, holding that on the facts of their two cases, her situation was not at all the same. First, in contrast to the earlier case, the search of Dr Fosh's computer had been authorised under the university's procedures. Secondly, since the earlier case had been decided, Parliament had passed the Regulation of Investigatory Powers Act 2000, which sets out in considerable detail the circumstances under which electronic surveillance may be authorised by criminal investigators and others. The EAT felt no need to address whether these searches had been authorised under that Act.

Although the EAT found that Dr Fosh's dismissal was fair, there is something troubling about this part of its decision. The university has searched through emails which Dr Fosh could reasonably have considered private, and treated relatively minor misconduct as a dismissal offence. This was not a case where some well-advertised harm had taken place and the university was doing no more than diligently seeking to identify the culprit. None of her former students had complained about Dr Fosh's emails regarding her line manager. Without having searched her email account, the university would not have known that she had done anything wrong. The logic of the process was about constructing a case against Dr Fosh after a decision had already been taken to dismiss her. To find, as the Tribunal did, that there had been no infringement at all of her right to respect for her private and family life, her home, or even her correspondence is clearly wrong.

Unfortunately, the typical experience of the Tribunal litigant is well encapsulated by these two cases. For while both Mr Dooley and Dr Fosh could say that there were merits to parts of their cases, ultimately, both lost. A Tribunal claimant winning *because* of the Human Rights Act is rare indeed.

There are a number of factors which together help to explain the undramatic impact of the Act and the Convention: employment law tends to raise issues of social and economic rights[34] which are not addressed in the European Convention but feature in other European documents such as the European Social Charter. The Court's key task in the present period is to foster the development of a culture of respect for political rights in the former Iron Curtain states where such rights have shallow roots. It intervenes with force to protect political rights and the right to a fair trial. But as there is a very wide range of domestic practice between contracting states in important areas of employment law such as trade union rights, it is harder for the Court to take an interventionist line. A number of rights such as the right not to suffer discrimination are better protected in the law of the European Union than they are in the Convention, so where our employment law produces a manifest injustice, claimants have sought to have their cases referred to the

European Court of Justice located in Luxembourg rather than the Court of Human Rights in Strasbourg.[35]

It may be that part of the difficulty is that economic relationships are so pervasive and of such fundamental importance to our society that Judges are likely to show an even greater deference to the authorities than they do even in the admittedly hierarchical worlds of crime, family and housing.

An additional factor may be the status of the Tribunal as a court created by statute in contrast to (for example) the High Court, the Court of Appeal, or the Supreme Court. Being the creature of statute, the Tribunal can only hear a case if Parliament has specifically reserved for it the power to do so. So, for example, although they arise in an employment setting, because there is no power reserving them to the Tribunal, the Tribunal cannot in general hear personal injury claims arising from accidents at work. These can only be brought in the County Court or the High Court.

Section 4 of the HRA gives certain courts the power to declare that statutes are incompatible with the European Convention. The High Court has this power, as does the Court of Appeal and the Supreme Court. The Tribunal does not have this power; neither does the EAT. The most striking omission is the Appeal Tribunal. The EAT is largely staffed by Circuit Judges. When they are in the High Court, they sit alone. When they sit in the EAT, they have the additional benefit of experienced Tribunal lay members who sit with them. There is no obvious reason why a Judge sitting in the EAT should lack powers that he has when sitting in the High Court.[36]

The immediate effect of the exclusion in section 4 is that a claimant complaining that the legislation governing her claim is incompatible with the Convention has to wait until her case has reached the Court of Appeal before she can make this point directly. This rather than the generosity of employment legislation explains why employment law has never seen the sustained campaign that led, for example, to the victory of tenants in the case of *Manchester* v *Pinnock*. The powerlessness of the employment courts to make a declaration of incompatibility has an impact on their willingness to read legislation purposively (a power they do have).

In the context of the several obstacles to workers' rights which are represented by the day-to-day practice of the employment courts, this is another small but definite barrier ensuring that workers leave the Tribunal dissatisfied.

7
Unions and the Law

If somebody says to me as [an Employment Judge] 'what do you know of industrial relations?' I say 'I don't know very much because it's a very complicated subject but as regards conditions in industry I find I know about industry in general rather more than the average trade union officer ... I have been sitting full time for four years, a year or two before that part-time, every day dealing with instances in somebody's working life and one goes into all kinds of occupations and the average union officer knows an awful lot about his own industry but he does not know a large amount about the others.[1]

Industrial Tribunals have nothing to do with the decision as to whether or not a worker is victimised or made redundant. These issues are resolved by the balance of forces between trade unions and employers. Tribunals can only set a price on what is an accomplished fact and even then only within certain limits. The fight for trade union rights has to be carried on at the bargaining table and on the picket line, not in the Tribunal rooms. However, if you have exhausted all trade union methods to influence the decision at issue, understanding that Tribunal remedies are second best, then there is nothing wrong with ensuring that compensation is as high as possible.[2]

In January 2009, Karen Reissmann, a sacked mental health nurse and UNISON activist, brought a claim of unfair dismissal to the Tribunal. Reissmann said that she had been dismissed by her employer for whistleblowing. Around 700 workers at her Trust had taken strike action for 14 days in an attempt to save her job. The Tribunal hearing lasted for full two days. The Employment Judge made a number of rulings which had the effect of narrowing the scope of Reissmann's claim. On the third day of the hearing, the case was compromised, with the settlement agreement including a confidentiality clause binding on both parties. The left-wing press took up the story:

> In a statement ... Karen said that she was 'happy with the outcome of the case'. She also pointed out that, in general, Employment Tribunals reflect a system that benefits employers.

> She said, 'About 87 percent of cases brought to Tribunal are won by employers.[3] And, even if you win your case, Tribunals do not have the power to demand your reinstatement.'
>
> The problems in the Tribunal system are a matter for the whole trade union movement.[4]

This book has already made the point that the present Tribunal system is the work of policy makers, chief among them the labour lawyer Otto Kahn-Freund. One part of Kahn-Freund's argument, as we have seen, was that an expanded Tribunal system would most likely result in greater industrial peace. For at least some commentators, the UK's present Employment Tribunal system is the shadow of the country's previous history of union militancy. Thus J.R. Shackleton writes:

> The subduing of the unions has been seen by admirers of the Thatcher governments as one of their greatest achievements, the fulfilment of a desire going back many years. But folklore tells us to be careful what we wish for: those who get their wishes granted often find they have got something they did not quite bargain for. The new focus on individual rights manifested in the growth of tribunal applications is the flipside of the decline in union power.[5]

Now it would be possible to place on a single graph two lines showing the increase in the number of Tribunal claims since 1971 and the decrease in the number of strikes over the same period and to conclude mechanically from this graph that the rising number of legal claims is the primary explanation for the falling number of strikes. Yet such an over-simplistic approach must be wrong. People are not the prisoners of legal relationships, they respond flexibly to legal opportunity according to a judgment of their interest and in the context of longer historical and political dynamics which make individual litigation appear more or less sensible at different times. One document cited in an earlier chapter was a survey conducted by the Ministry of Labour of unofficial strikes, listed by the cause of strike (see Table 7.1).

Looking at these same categories again, it is clear that many of them (for example wages, hours of work, and even working arrangements) continue to be taken up as issues by trade unions in a fashion which has not changed much since the 1960s. Other areas however (redundancy, disciplinary and 'other individual' cases) have entered the legal sphere over the past 40 years, and in the majority of workplaces are now dealt with as legal matters (that is, by individual casework by a union representative, backed up by the threat of Tribunal action) rather than by strikes.

Table 7.1 Number of unofficial strikes in 1965, by cause[6]

Wages	1,173
Hours of work	22
Demarcation	59
Redundancy	51
Individual disciplinary	131
Other individual	150
Working arrangements	761
Trade union recognition	28
Closed shop	32
Victimisation for union membership	13
Trade union status	8
Sympathy disputes	26
Total	2,454

In a context where the major causes of strike activity in the 1960s continue to be resolved by industrial relations rather than litigation, it follows that by far the most important explanations for the decline in the number of strikes have nothing at all to do with the trend towards litigation of individual employment disputes. More important are the legacy of the unions' setbacks in the battles of the 1980s, the anti-union laws adopted in the same period, and the failure of such union victories as there have been in recent years to give such confidence to workers as to transform the mood in the workplace.[7] If the use of the law to resolve employment disputes can be added to this picture, it remains a subsidiary explanation.

The more interesting part of the relationship between strikes and Employment Tribunal figures is the other side of the coin: the extent to which the rising figures of Employment Tribunal claims show that workers continue to have grievances at work, even when strikes are low. Put like this, Tribunal figures can be taken as a barometer of the remaining strong sense of many employees that work itself is a hostile environment characterised by unequal power relationships which require the intervention of an outside force to prevent unfair treatment.

From the above analysis, it follows that any plans to reduce the number of Tribunal claims, without intervening in the structural relationship of inequality between workers and managers, will be utopian at best and malign at worst. Tribunal claims are running at this high level because there are imbalances of power in the workplaces which make disputes inevitable, and more specifically because of the partial effectiveness of the strategy of juridification of employment disputes that was applied in 1971. Short of actually penalising workers who bring employment claims, the only process that could achieve a lasting reduction in the number of Tribunal disputes would be for workers themselves to take their grievances back out of the legal sphere, and to raise them directly as matters for collective protest at work. Yet this would be the worst scenario for employers.

UNIONS AND THE FUNDING OF TRIBUNAL CLAIMS

In a context of increasing claims, the temptation for unions is to market themselves to members as specialist insurance schemes, offering the expectation of legal cover where a member of the union is subject to a detriment at work. A difficulty of this approach is that unions are wary of charging high fees (most unions charge around £100–120 per year for most categories of membership). Beyond litigation, they have many other calls on their membership fees; and only a relatively small proportion of a union budget will be set aside for legal representation.

Table 7.2 Unions, by membership and expenditure on legal funds in 2008 (selection)[8]

Communication Workers Union	230,968	£322,373 = £1.40 per member
Unite the Union	1,635,483	£4,814,000 = £2.94 per member
GMB	601,131	£2,089,000 = £3.48 per member
Equity	36,441	£135,994 = £3.73 per member
British Dental Association	23,496	£116,424 = £4.96 per member
National Union of Journalists	36,081	£401,789 = £11.14 per member

The above figures do not compare like with like. It is certainly not the case, for example, that members of the National Union of Journalists have access to ten times more by way of legal services than their counterparts in the Communication Workers Union (CWU). The CWU has a full-time legal office staffed by more than a dozen employees, who act as solicitors for CWU members. The union is able to provide services in a wide range of areas, including personal injury claims, clinical negligence claims, criminal injuries compensation cases, and criminal defence. The costs of employing full-time solicitors appear in the union budgets under the general costs of employing ordinary staff (and not in the budgets for legal services). The costs borne by the CWU and shown in Table 7.2 above arise from atypical and complex cases, or cases that require especially skilled outside advice. The National Union of Journalists by contrast, being a much smaller union, does not employ full-time legal officers, but has a referral scheme with the solicitors Thompsons. The figure given for the NUJ's legal expenses per member is a much more complete picture of the *total* legal costs faced by any trade union. Moreover, the National Union of Journalists is a specialist union. The union takes active steps to restrict membership to bona fide journalists. Members receive legal assistance in a much wider group of cases than simply tribunal claims (including, for example, claims over copyright, as well as the drafting of contracts in non-employment situations). It would be unrealistic anyway to focus on the costs faced by any one union in just a single year, especially a relatively small union, as its costs may be skewed by even small numbers of one-off claims.[9]

Even with these notes of caution in mind, it is striking that none of the unions in the above list was spending more than £12 on legal fees per member per year. In 1985, it was estimated that of all workers in the UK, 1.1 per cent are dismissed in any one year.[10] The economy has become more flexible since then, and as a very roughly estimate, the figure is now usually closer to 2 per cent, in other words one in 50 of all workers are dismissed in a typical year.[11] Even if a union was spending on average £12 per member per year on legal fees, and even if every penny of this fund was available to all its dismissed members (and the non-dismissed members were making no claim on this collective resource), it is still the case that the average union member would have access to a shared resource of the equivalent of just £600 to spend on legal fees. This is a very modest sum. It is only a quarter of the average sum spent by claimants on their dispute, or one-tenth of the sum spent by respondents.[12] It might not cover a single day's representation at the Tribunal, and it certainly would not cover a full day's hearing plus the necessary advance preparation of the case.[13] Once we also factor in the context that any union must cover a very wide range of employment disputes, of which dismissals are only a small proportion; that most unions must pay for non-employment litigation as well (as in the examples of the National Union of Journalists and the Communication Workers Union above); and indeed that unions are membership networks of lay representatives who must be trained and are supported by regional and national officials who have to be employed, and do not work primarily as lawyers, it will become clear that the unions, simply to avoid bankrupting themselves, find themselves turning down many worthwhile applications for legal support.

Sarah Veale, the Head of Equality and Employment Rights Department at the Trades Union Congress, describes the total process well:

> Strengthening individual employment rights has been transforming labour relations in a way that is not necessarily beneficial to union organisation. That is not to say that employees should not have individual rights of course. My concern is that the increasing individualisation of employment rights, coupled with reductions in trade union rights, has led to a situation where unions have less and less bargaining power and have to act mainly as representatives of individuals, rather than tackling workplace problems collectively. As unions were designed to act as collective representatives they are not always able to handle more than a limited number of individual grievances and problems in the workplace; they can then be seen as weak by workers and not worth the subscription costs.[14]

This process can be tracked more closely by looking at some of the ways individual unions have dealt with the problem of allocating legal resources.

CASE STUDY: RACE AND THE AUT

In 2004, a consultant, Harminder Singh, led an inquiry into the legal services provided to its black members by the Association of University Teachers (AUT), then one of the two main unions representing lecturers in higher education. Of course, in many ways higher education is an unusual sector.[15] Average wages of full-time employees are significantly higher than the UK average; while the sector also has some of the highest rates of casual employment of any parts of the UK economy, with the result that very many teaching staff are paid wages of less than £5,000 per year. Moreover, the conditions of black lecturers (compared to white lecturers) appear to show much higher levels of institutional discrimination than is apparent in other parts of the economy. So, while around one-tenth of all college and university lecturers are black, just 0.4 per cent of all university professors are black.[16] This picture provides some of the context to Singh's report. Black members of the AUT were campaigning for a greater use of strategic litigation. Singh was asked to investigate whether such a strategy would be practicable for the union or even desirable.

Singh began by describing the steps of litigation. At the first stage, a member of the union would approach a representative of their Local Association (LA). The representative would then have a choice: either to seek to resolve the matter within the organisation, usually by raising a grievance or an appeal against the employer, or by seeking external resolution. Where the representative agreed to take up the worker's claim, he did so, Singh suggested, at the risk of cost to himself. Representatives are not paid for their service, but work at lunch-hours and evenings. Representatives place themselves in the middle of disputes which are likely to be heated. The representative may be seen by their managers to be a troublemaker. If their advice is unsuccessful, or if they let the claimant down, they too may be tarred with racism. 'It would appear to benefit all concerned', Harminder Singh writes, 'to take the court-based approach. The LA representative takes the risk-free route. The black member gets the help of an expert in race discrimination legislation.'[17]

At a second stage, the union would decide whether or not to fund a claim to a Tribunal. The union's Legal Aid Rules presented assistance as a right: 'The association offers a comprehensive legal service to members.' In Singh's words: 'the expectation is that members need to do nothing to solve their own workplace problems because the AUT provides this as a service and, in any event, the representatives can be bypassed to get individual legal advice without limit.'[18] Because of the considerable complexity of race discrimination claims, Singh estimated that the typical expense to the union in bringing a race claim was around £30,000, and the typical pay-out (where successful) was £5,000. It should also be said that a typical AUT member at that time contributed around £150 each year to the union by way of membership fees. The policy of the AUT at the time was to support only claims which had a better than 50 per cent chance of success. Yet as we have seen, the actual average success rate of race claims at Tribunal is closer to one in six. Inevitably, the union would support only a minority of the claims that were proposed for funding. Inevitably also, the union was regularly turning down some claims which high street solicitors would have taken on, say, on a no-win no-fee basis.

At a third stage, employers would often offer a settlement to a member as a means of avoiding a hearing: at the time Singh's document was written, roughly one-fifth of all race claims reached a final hearing, with a majority being settled or withdrawn. Singh chided AUT members for having exaggerated expectations of the courts:

> When we read of successful Tribunal claims in the media it portrays a story that brings satisfaction: a just cause, fighting for principles, taking victory in a dignified way whilst the losers are publicly shamed for the unconscionable behaviour with the courts underlining this with large six-figure compensation awards.[19]

Hopes were inevitably dashed when the union recommended the acceptance of an employer's offer: 'The member may appear, to the advisor, to be unreasonably unwilling to accept what appears to be a "generous" or "realistic" settlement. The member may feel the union or its advisors have not tried hard enough.'[20]

At a fourth stage, those cases which were not settled (and which the union agreed to continue to support) were heard by the Tribunal. Some were won, but others lost. Even where the union member remained in post, Singh suggested, the effect of having brought a case was to permanently distance the member from the Local Association: 'It makes it more difficult for the LA representative to give assistance at this stage, as reasons for losing are sought within the legal framework, e.g. wanting a black solicitor, or a second opinion from counsel.'[21]

Singh's document was published by the union. Its message was ostensibly downbeat: expectations needed to be lowered, if the union was to survive. One point Singh highlighted was that members of unions seeking legal assistance inevitably take more from the pooled resources of the union than they give. Race claims are heard over more days than other Tribunal claims and have unusually high costs, but even a relatively simple unfair dismissal claim – with external representation – will probably cost the union as much as the member will pay in a lifetime of fees. Legal advice is rationed and, more to the point, it can often *feel* rationed.

CLAIMS AGAINST UNIONS

One purpose of Harminder Singh's document was to discourage union members from over-reliance on litigation. He stressed the problems of litigation for members, for union representatives, and for the collective culture of the union. One problem Singh did not address was the potential for union members to sue their own union.

But logically, this must be one risk of the trend towards the individualisation of employment rights. Members of unions have long had the power to sue their union in High Court or to bring a case to the Certification Officer where a union uses its property unlawfully, or where a union fails to hold fair elections.[22] Historically, the scope for unions to be sued for mistakes made when representing their members was limited; but the ability to sue a union has been widened in recent years by the use of the anti-discrimination laws, which apply to unions as they do to employers.

In *British Medical Association* v *Chaudhury*, the claimant was an NHS registrar, a post from which it is possible to be promoted to consultant status. In 1991, Mr Chaudhury accepted a post of registrar in urology at North Manchester General Hospital. The advertisement stated that the post was 'Royal College approved'. In 1996, by which time he was working in Portsmouth, Mr Chaudhury applied to gain transition to a new specialist registrar grade. His application was rejected, essentially because the relevant professional body had in the interim decided that the Manchester hospital was not suitable for higher specialist training. Mr Chaudhury applied to the British Medical Association (BMA), which is the nearest thing to a trade union for GPs and doctors in hospitals, for legal support in a race discrimination complaint against the authorities in Portsmouth. The BMA declined his application. In 1997, Mr Chaudhury submitted a number of complaints to various bodies, including a claim to the Employment Tribunal against the BMA. The Tribunal held that had the BMA supported his claims they would have had a 50 per cent chance of success. Had he been successful, Mr Chaudhury would have been appointed to a consultant's position. In 2002, the Tribunal awarded Mr Chaudhury £814,877.41, then the largest sum ever to have been awarded to any claimant in any race case. Unfortunately for Mr Chaudhury, his case ended rather less happily. The BMA appealed to the EAT and the case was eventually heard by the Court of Appeal. Ten years after he submitted his original application to the Tribunal, the Court found for the BMA,[23] and Mr Chaudhury was left with nothing except (presumably) a very large legal bill.

Odd as it may sound, when describing a closely reasoned judgment that ran to no less than 252 paragraphs, the Court of Appeal did not particularly consider the extent of the duty that a union owed to its member (in particular, where the union was accused of indirect discrimination), beyond using the common law's general term of convenience, 'reasonableness'. The British Medical Association had been right not to support Mr Chaudhury, the Court found, as his race claim against the authorities in Portsmouth had no realistic prospect of success. The BMA's refusal to support Mr Chaudhury was 'reasonable' and it was therefore not discriminatory.[24]

Another case heard in 2007 concerned a lecturer, Mr D'Silva, whose union the National Association of Teachers in Further and High Education (NATFHE) had merged in 2006 with Harminder Singh's union the Association of University Teachers, to form a new union, the University and Colleges Union (UCU).[25] Mr D'Silva's case arose from his membership of NATFHE. In 2005, he approached NATFHE for support with a claim of race victimisation against his employer, arising from a failure of the employer to provide him with a suitable reference. Mr D'Silva ascribed this failure to victimisation, following a previous complaint which he had made against the employer, which had ultimately been compromised. Under NATFHE's legal assistance scheme, members had no general right to legal assistance, but assistance might be granted with reference to a number of key criteria, including prospects of success, the potential of a claim to impact positively upon other members of the union, and the likely costs of a claim. The hearing for which Mr D'Silva wanted support was scheduled to last 14 days. NATFHE has employees who are in-house specialist employment solicitors and the union also sometimes calls on barristers in complex cases. The union's senior solicitor advised that the claim had less than a 50 per cent chance of success. At Mr D'Silva's prompting however, a further meeting was sought with counsel. Again, the advice was that prospects were poor. There followed an exchange of letters, with Mr D'Silva threatening to take legal action against the union. NATFHE then formally declined assistance, whereupon Mr D'Silva commenced an Employment Tribunal claim for indirect discrimination against the union. He was unsuccessful at the Tribunal and on appeal.

There are two aspects of the case which are of interest. First, this was another race claim that broke (in common with several other cases that have been described earlier in this book) on the rock of the reversed burden of proof. The claimant pointed to facts which he said were in his favour. The trade union did not collect data to show how it treated different categories of applicant to its legal assistance scheme. Mr D'Silva requested this data in a race questionnaire but the union was unable to provide it. He pointed to other white members who did receive assistance from the union and complained that when he had sought detailed information about their cases the union had declined to disclose it. The EAT held that there was no evidence for the burden of proof to pass: 'there was nothing in the circumstances of the case that raised even a *prima facie* case of discrimination.'[26]

Secondly, on its facts, the case gives an insight into the contrast between members' expectations of unions and the actual performance of unions as employment litigators. Long before Mr D'Silva's relationship with NATFHE had broken down, it was already showing tensions. Mr D'Silva specifically requested a barrister from one particular chambers, Littleton. Their barristers were unavailable at a price that the union could afford. Against the advice of the barrister recommended by NATFHE, Mr D'Silva relied on a favourable opinion he had received from the Council for Ethnic Minority (CEM), which according to its own website is a

> ... voluntary organisation based in London but its services to professional, non-professional and other victims are extended throughout the United Kingdom and overseas. The CEM provides confidential advice for a collective fight against all forms of discrimination in the Higher Education & other sectors.[27]

It is a lobbying organisation rather than a collective of experienced lawyers.

Mr D'Silva complained that the barrister obtained for less than a Littleton barrister lacked experience of race discrimination cases. He wanted a second opinion from 'more senior' counsel. He complained in his letters that despite ten years' membership of the union he had not 'received value for money as have other ethnic minorities'. It seems very likely that other black members of the union could have been found who shared his complaints; even though Mr Silva's claim was wholly unsuccessful both at the Tribunal and on appeal.

EQUAL PAY

We have already seen in the earlier chapter on equal pay some of the dangers of the juridification of individual employment disputes. One case which shows the limitations of the partnership approach was *GMB* v *Allen*, heard in the Employment Appeal Tribunal in February 2007 and in the Court of Appeal in May 2008. Like many recent high-profile employment cases, it was an equal pay claim.

What distinguished the case was that the claimants blamed not their employer but their union for pay inequality.

The claimants were five women employees of Middlesbrough Council, whose employees had been subject to a regrading exercise, in which it was found that several categories of worker had been underpaid. These workers received pay rises. Other groups of workers had their pay cut. The question remained of what would happen to workers who had been paid less. Could they bring claims for their past six years of unequal pay? Council managers offered the union a deal under which these workers were divided in two groups. One group would receive roughly a quarter of the potential value of their claim. The other group would receive nothing at all. The union's bargaining difficulties were described in the EAT in the following terms:

> The union, therefore, was faced with a situation where the interests of those women with historic equal pay claims would be served by pressing those claims and also by seeking to secure the backdating of pay up to the six years permitted by law to redress past discriminatory wrongs. As against that, they had to seek to provide pay protection for those who would otherwise have had their pay reduced following the implementation of the single status agreement; and they wished to improve pay for the future for all their members.
>
> In relation to these conflicting objectives, the union also had to have regard to the fact that the council did not have unlimited resources. As the Tribunal found, there was a genuine fear that if the union pressed too hard for the interests of the women seeking back pay for past discrimination, it could undermine the aim to maximise pay protection and secure pay increases for the future. In addition, the Tribunal accepted that the union were genuinely concerned that pushing too hard for back pay might possibly lead to redundancies or contracting-out by the council in order to enable it to meet its liabilities. Neither was an attractive option for the union or its members.[28]

The eventual outcome of the case was that the Court of Appeal found that the union had indirectly discriminated against its members. It had applied a practice of agreeing to a low back pay settlement for certain groups of workers in order to leave as much money as possible for the pay protection of other workers (who were predominantly male) and for the future pay of all workers. This policy had discriminated against women. It had not been justified. Although this is not entirely clear from the judgment, the key fact which impressed the members of the Court (or so it appeared when watching the hearing from the public gallery) was the *time* taken by the union in reaching a decision to accept the first offer put to them by management, which the Tribunal had analysed as follows:

> [The Union] rushed headlong into accepting an ill-considered back pay deal accepting the Council's plea of poverty without question ... The Union did not take any advice or probe the Council in any way to see whether, although there may not have been a provision in their budget for the making of any more substantial back pay settlement, they could raise the money by the selling of capital assets or by making savings in areas other than payroll. Very little care indeed went into the assessment of the back offer.[29]

There were other factual matters which weighed against the union. In particular, the union had misrepresented the terms of the arrangement to its members, giving the impression that the women concerned were getting a good deal, when in reality they were being asked to make sacrifices on behalf of other workers.

At the Tribunal, the GMB was found to have discriminated against the women concerned, and this decision was reaffirmed by the Court of Appeal. The case has (we must assume) made it easier for other claimants to bring cases against unions, especially where a union has failed to represent its members properly, or where it has sold a proposed agreement to its members on a false basis. It may even make it easier for dissatisfied members to bring claims against lay trade union representatives. No trade union in the UK is doing enough, even now, to train or support representatives in what are increasingly complex areas of the law.

In *Allen*, the Tribunal criticised the union for it termed 'aporia', meaning a state of indecision caused by an apparently insoluble problem. The issue of equal pay had been there for union representatives to see for a decade. The closer that the need for a decision approached, the more the union ceded the initiative to management. The result, ultimately, was a successful case against the union.

What the GMB should have done, of course, is campaign against the high salaries pervasive among council managers, using the single-status negotiations as an opportunity to renegotiate the pay structure in favour of lower-paid grades. Such tactics could have resulted in both pay protection and more equal pay. But in order to be successful, the employer would have had to accept that several of its senior employees would be paid less in future; and it would only have done this if it felt under real threat from a union serious about a more combative approach.

A more militant strategy would not merely raise the possibility of a different outcome in terms of local government pay, it could also usefully be offered as an alternative to the over-litigation of individual disputes, especially dismissals. Where these have been seen as automatically grounds for a strike ballot, the affected workers' chances of avoiding dismissal or securing reinstatement have been much greater than where the union concedes to the employer in practice the right to dismiss and relies on the Tribunal to provide financial recompense.

Few readers will be unaware that for most of the past three decades in Britain the number of strikes has been falling. At the same time, the number of union representatives has declined, as has the density of union membership and the coverage in the press of industrial bargaining. Yet there are plausible reasons to think that the weakening of unions since the mid-1970s may be coming to an end.

First, unions are social movements, and like all movements they are organised by activists, who are volunteers. Even today, many union branches are led by representatives who have a collective memory of defeat. In Britain, with the defeat of the miners in 1984–85, because the strike lasted so long, and because the state took part with such an extraordinary show of force (jailing strikers in their dozens, and sequestering the union's funds), the unions suffered a dramatic setback, greater than any similar defeat elsewhere in the developed world at that time. There was nothing on the same scale in France, Germany, Spain, or Greece; and this helps to explain why even in the past two decades there have been repeated labour uprisings in Europe, which have not been accompanied by equivalent waves of strike action here. Britain, which 30 or 40 years ago was commonly seen as one of the most strike-prone countries in Europe, is now seen as having a relatively docile labour force. The further we get from 1984–85, the weaker the memory of defeat will be, and the greater the opportunity for new generation of activists to emerge.

Secondly, the various limitations on the right to strike that were enshrined in legislation in the 1980s, had as their intended beneficiary the litigious user of public services, having no interest in the dispute save for the continuity of whatever service it was that the consumer relied on when the workers were not on strike. The last decade has seen few examples of such private litigants, eager to sue strikers at British Airways (BA) or on the London Underground or wherever. This was noticeable in 2010 and 2011, when the High Court and then the Court of Appeal repeatedly had to consider the compliance of various striking unions with the balloting requirements set out in statute. Where the employers sued, relying on various technical breaches of the strike rules, the Judges had real difficulty in understanding the purpose of the legislation which they were supposed to interpret. 'Why does the law require unions to publicise the number of workers who spoil their ballot papers in a strike ballot?', Lady Justice Smith asked David Reade, counsel for BA in the Court of Appeal. The evident difficulty that he had in discerning any purpose to the legislation (beyond the simple, brute, desire of a previous generation of legislators to prevent strikes), found its expression in due course in a decision of the court not to enforce legislation which the Judges had no good reason to read in the employers' favour.[30] The long hostility of the higher courts to union organisation, detailed elsewhere in this book, is not yet at an end. The suffocation of the past over the present may however be starting to lift.

Third, the emergent forms of technology in recent years have been unusually hostile to labour organisation.[31] The point is best understood by comparing the last 40 years with the earlier decades of the last century. In the 1900s and 1910s, the newest and most important forms of industry were giant metal works capable of producing heavy industrial goods. These were characterised by a concentration of labour in large workplaces, which then became the pattern in the economy generally. The numbers of workers employed in a typical workplace were large, the workers were employed in similar roles, and the dynamics of industrial management ensured a rigid divide between workers and managers, in which the former had many reasons to regard their interests as different from those of their employers.

In the 1950s and 1960s, there was a similar dynamic, by which the light industrial habits of the car factory were adopted throughout the economy. These waves of technology again produced relatively large workplaces with many workers doing similar tasks and relatively small numbers of workers in management positions. These were, once again, propitious circumstances in which trade unions were able to build a mass membership and negotiate improvements in millions of workers' lives.

In the last few decades, the emergent technologies have been computer-based; and even such 'old technologies' as transport and manufacture have been transformed by waves of automation which have dramatically reduced the numbers of workers required to produce or supply any given quantity of goods or services. The demographic relationship between labour and management in many workplaces has changed dramatically. There are relatively fewer workers, employed in more diverse roles. Managers constitute a larger proportion of the workforce than before. Management in general has been able to advance its position at labour's cost.

Computerisation has also had an impact on the costs of production, so that while in several countries wages have been static (real wages in the United States peaked in around 1975; while in the UK they peaked in around 2001), declining hourly pay has been offset by cheaper goods. In the most general terms, low inflation tends to produce weaker unions. Stronger unions have been built during periods of middling, not low, inflation, as in these circumstances workers are under greater pressure to organise to match their wages to rising prices.

All over Britain, industrial districts can be found which four decades ago were dominated by just one or two employers, and which in living memory employed tens of thousands of workers. In many cases, the factory is still there and the volume of production has increased but the number of workers there is reduced.

We have lived through a short industrial epoch which has been dramatically hostile to labour organising, but this moment stands out in contrast to the century that went before, and there is no reason to think that the recent trends will continue. While computer technology is enabling parts of the productive process to be done by smaller groups of workers, it is equally bringing together groups of workers in new roles often on a mass scale (for example, in call centres, or in transport hubs where very large numbers of workers are required to organise the distribution of goods purchased online). Computer technology in itself is a set of technological innovations, some of which are already proving favourable to union organising: as, for example, the role of social media in facilitating the 2011 revolts in North Africa and the Middle East, a significant component of which has been labour militancy.[32]

Fourth, for several years the signs have been that several staple goods (oil, cotton, cocoa, corn) are set on a secular trend of rising prices. The combination of pay freezes and rising inflation cannot be sustained indefinitely without protest.

Fifth, the cuts agenda of the Coalition government will force unions to resist what would otherwise be a devastating attack on their members' lives. Two surveys illustrate the extent of the challenge. A survey published by the Resolution Foundation in May 2011 used government forecasting data to show that real wages in the UK will be no higher in 2015 than they were in 2001.[33] Two months later, a survey commissioned by the Chartered Institute for Personnel and Development showed that one-half of all UK workers had seen their actual pay frozen or cut over the past twelve months;[34] and this against a background of inflation of 5 per cent (RPI).[35]

In short, the relationship between unions and the public (in general) is in motion. Those who take for granted that the last 30 years' pattern of shrinking union membership will continue, may well be surprised.

The argument of this book is that the best alternative to the legalisation of employment disputes would be a shift on the part of workers and unions to take these conflicts out of the legal sphere and to return them to the sphere of collective bargaining. But in a policy context where the pressure for the reduction in Tribunal claims comes from government and employers, this alternative cannot be applied to every dispute. Workers at present bring claims to the Tribunal because, on a realistic evaluation of the alternative opportunities provided (for example) by industrial action, they judge the Tribunals, bad as they are, to be their best option. The example of Karen Reissmann given at the start of this chapter illustrates some of the problems. It is not that Reissmann and her allies were unaware of the potential of industrial action or indeed of the weakness of claimants (in general terms) before the Tribunal. They pushed industrial action as far as it would go. A strategy of litigation was adopted late, only when it was clear that strikes would not win back Reissmann's job.

Yet if there was a general increase in workers' willingness to take industrial action then what is presently a long-term alternative – the removal of legal cases from the Tribunal, and their resolution by the more effective means of industrial democracy – could yet become a matter of immediate possibility.

8
The Common Law

English law is either common law, in other words, unwritten law such as existed at the time when statutes were first gathered and later collated by legal authorities; on the most important points this law is naturally uncertain and ambiguous; or else it is statute law, which consists of an infinite number of individual acts of Parliament gathered over five hundred years, which contradict each other and represent not a 'state of law', but a state of complete lawlessness. The barrister is everything here; anyone who has wasted a lot of his time on this legal jungle, on this chaos of contradictions, is all-powerful in an English law-court.[1]

There is a tendency among labour lawyers to regard the courts with suspicion. The perception is that the judges are hostile to the interests of workers, and particularly to the collective interests of workers in trade unions, and that they favour the interests of employers. There is considerable evidence to support this view.[2]

Many of the criticisms commonly levied against the Employment Tribunal are 'promethean', by which it is meant only that they are easy to identify and could be remedied by legislation. The logic behind this book is different. The intention here is to explain the logic of the system, the discreet values which influence Tribunals irrespective of who is the Judge or the merits of the case being heard. One common experience of unrepresented claimants is that they encounter a very high degree of *procedural* fairness from Employment Judges, which is unrelated to the Judge's perception of the likely merits of the case. This is the sort of observation that can only be demonstrated by brief examples of Tribunal practice:

> In a case where an unrepresented claimant was cross-examining a witness (his former manager): the claimant stopped the witness from answering questions and spoke over him. The witness could hardly speak. It felt almost as if the claimant was bullying him. The respondent was represented by a barrister who indicated with her body language her unhappiness and a desire to intervene. The Judge turned to the barrister, looking at her as a teacher might at an unruly pupil: 'No, Ms X-.' The barrister crouched down in her chair. The Judge allowed the claimant's questions to continue.

> At a pre-hearing review, on reading the papers which the claimant had put in to the Tribunal, her claim barely made any sense at all. Moreover, she appeared to have submitted the key parts of it so late that on any proper application of the rules, it was clearly out of time and could not be heard. The Judge allowed the claimant to continue, advising her that she really should sort out the defects in her case, and giving her a further fortnight to do so.

Had either of these claimants been interviewed afterwards for their thoughts on the merits of the Tribunal system, each would have probably said that they had a scrupulously fair Judge, while each respondent had genuine grounds for complaint. But there is a sting in the tale. *In each of the cases, the Tribunal ultimately found in favour of the respondent and against the claimant.* Interim rulings may have helped the claimant, but were a poor guide to the outcome of the case.

Through this book, considerable weight has been put on the initial founding of the Tribunal system by the Industrial Relations Act 1971, following the Donovan Commission. It has been argued that these origins provided a negative legacy to the Tribunal. But to get at contradictory, day-to-day experiences of this character, some additional analysis must be made of the ongoing legal context – that is, the common law[3] – in which Employment Tribunal decisions are made.

Employment Tribunals inherit two legacies from the common law. The first is the memory of specific employment decisions made in a different epoch, when employment law did not exist and the courts recognised only masters and servants. The second is the much broader value system of the common law.

THE COMMON LAW AND CONTRACTS OF SERVICE

The most distinctive feature of the common law system, as opposed to, for example, constitutional legal systems, is that decisions are made on the basis of previous judgments, rather than by working from first principles from a list of constitutional principles. Common law lawyers will tell you that there are advantages to a system in which precedent conquers. It makes the law predictable. It removes the scope for the individual judge to make a ruling on a whim. In the words of Lord Edmund-Davies:

> Justice that pays no regard to precedent can be positively injustice ... I would struggle might and main to differentiate between a line of existing cases and the instant case in order to arrive at a just conclusion. But if there really is no substantial difference between the case I have in hand and earlier cases I cannot, consistent with my duty, forget those earlier cases ... Because I think that if you do not adopt that approach, chaos can result, and chaos and justice in my view are ill neighbours.[4]

Yet where the trend of statutory development is towards the creation of increased rights for specific groups of civil litigants, one danger of a common law system is that decisions made in a previous epoch (where the legal regime was more hostile) will be duplicated even in a period where statute is more friendly.

One instance of this problem having an effect on present-day employment law is the rule that a dismissed claimant has no remedy for the manner in which she was dismissed. So, for example, where an employer (A) dismisses employees (B) and (C), treating (B) with politeness and candour, but addressing (C) in a violent and demeaning fashion and causing considerable distress to (C), the courts will treat (B) and (C) as identical for the purpose of remedy; (C) has no additional claim.[5]

The origins of this rule lie in the old employment case of *Addis v Gramophone*, which predates the creation of Tribunals by more than 50 years. *Addis* was a wrongful dismissal case; in other words, a claim for damages where a worker complained that he was entitled to and had been paid notice pay. In *Addis,* a manager was dismissed on the grounds of allegations of fraud which were untrue. In the High Court, he was awarded damages of £600, including an element of additional compensation for false accusations that had been made during the dismissal. On the facts of the case, the House of Lords upheld the amount of damages. But on the question of principle, their Lordships ruled 5–1 against the possibility that a claimant was entitled to damages for the manner of their dismissal. The clearest statement of the majority position was delivered by Lord Shaw:

> A certain regret which accompanies the conclusion which I have reached on the facts of this particular case is abated by the consciousness that the settlement by your Lordships' House of the important question of principle and practice may go some length in preventing the intrusion of not a few matters

> of prejudice hitherto introduced for the inflation of damages in cases of wrongful dismissal and now definitely declared to be irrelevant ... .[6]

Such an argument can be well paraphrased in the following terms: the courts had never allowed damages of this sort before; the Lords saw no reason to start now.

To understand the mind-set of the judges who reached the decision in *Addis*, it should be remembered that in the years of their birth, the most important workplace statute had been the Master and Servant Act 1823.[7] This was a punitive measure that specified three months' hard labour for workers who absented themselves from work without notice. Admittedly, the Master and Servant Act 1867 which followed was more liberal. It contained punishments for either managers or workers who broke employment contracts. Yet the implementation of the law remained unbalanced. Willibald Steinmetz, a distinguished historian of employment litigation in the nineteenth century, observes that between 1868 and 1872, only six employers were sentenced under the Act. By contrast, in the same period, some 495 employees were sentenced to imprisonment for breaches of contract.[8] Only with the passage of the Employers and Workmen Act 1875 did courts lose the ability to jail employees for breaches.[9] The judges who found that there should be no compensation for the manner of dismissal were themselves barely catching up with a whole epoch of labour legislation. It is perhaps less surprising that they reached the decision that they did, than that Tribunals continue to treat *Addis* as an authority.[10]

The Asymmetries of the Common Law

Having mentioned his work, Steinmetz is a useful guide to follow further, because the question which dominates his work is one which is of interest to this project too (although the period he studies admittedly is very different from our own). Steinmetz observes that between 1823 and 1914, the trend of employment statute law was to increase the rights of workers. The Act of 1867 was more progressive than the Act of 1823. The 1875 Act was more liberal still. Indeed, the last significant pre-*Addis* statute was the Trades Disputes Act 1906, which removed unions' liability for economic torts arising from strikes (and was far more permissive than the law that we have today).

The system became more just to employees. Yet this period was also characterised by a tendency of workers to avoid litigation where possible. In his research, Steinmetz cites the evidence of 15 county courts from across Britain, including Bow, Kettering and Gateshead. These were courts where workers might bring claims for physical injuries suffered during employment, or claims for breaches of contract such as wrongful dismissal. Steinmetz shows that after 1871, the number of employment cases fell in each of these courts. He estimates that employment cases represented around one in 50 county court cases in 1880, and only one in 200, 30 years later.[11] Fairer laws did not reverse the trend for employment to take up less time in court. The Trades Disputes Act provided for conciliation between unions and employers. The total number of cases that came to industrial conciliation boards however was low; at around 2,000 between 1890 and 1910.[12] By 1925 to 1928, these boards were dealing with almost no cases at all. In Germany, by contrast, the industrial tribunals (*Gewerbegerichte*) and workers' courts (*Arbeitsgerichte*) saw a rising number of cases, with the former addressing 69,000 cases in 1896, 111,000 in 1907, 169,000 in 1925, and the latter adjudicating in 300,000 cases a year by 1928.[13]

In the period Steinmetz studies, the law became significantly more open to workers yet there was no increase in the number of employment cases. To explain this paradox, Steinmetz looked at the arbitration committees that were developed after 1906, and showed that the strategy of the unions *vis-à-vis* these conciliation mechanisms was to use them to generate national policies, rather than resolve individual cases.[14] Individuals were often badly served by this process, Steinmetz argues, as unions tended to use the individual cases as subordinate examples of general issues requiring policy change. Employers and trade unions cooperated in the removal of the law as a mechanism for the resolution of individual disputes.

If the law became more liberal, then why did this not result in a 're-juridification' of industrial relations? Here Steinmetz makes an original claim: that any individual's experience of employment law is under-determined by the content of legislation and over-determined by the residual structures of the law. The implied contrast is with the German labour courts, which had a statutory duty to attempt conciliation, which excluded lawyers from hearings, and which did not allow appeals to the higher courts. The application of justice was simpler as well as more amenable to the worker. British law was characterised by high costs to the litigant, delays in providing redress, risks of dismissal, and an inadequate supply of lawyers or insurance.

In an important passage, Steinmetz writes of the 'hidden asymmetries' of the law:

> English law was (and is) characterized by a distinction before two normative concepts, statute law and common law. This dualistic structure of legislative and judicial power favoured the employers in very many cases. Since the statutes often only defined very vaguely such central terms as 'servant' or the different forms of the contract, the standards of the common law had to be consulted.[15]

The language of English law was both too simple and too complex to resolve workers' disputes. The common law was over-simple: it imported abstract concepts such as a rule that promises (contracts) must be honoured. In the hierarchical world of the English workplace, these rules tended to work for the employer, who drafted the original contract. It was the employee's promise to the employer that usually was broken. On the other hand, the complexity of statute also tended to disadvantage the employee, with its multiple competing definitions of words such as 'servant'. Strained once more through the collective values of the judges, the outcome was unpredictable at best.[16] It was not the bias so much as the complexity and especially the uncertainty of the common law system which, Steinmetz argues, encouraged workers to look elsewhere for the redress of grievances.

Applying these same concepts to the present, it could certainly be said that the defining legacy of common law to employment litigation is indeed a tradition of complexity and uncertainty. Even in *Addis*, when employment law was in its infancy, the House of Lords were able to cite 15 relevant cases in a judgment of 6,000 words. The complexity is not merely a matter of inherited concepts but reflects an idea of what the law ought to be, which continues to shape the drafters of legislation. More than 30 years ago, Lord Denning complained, 'If we are not careful we shall find industrial tribunals bent down under the weight of law books or, what is worse, asleep under them.'[17] For all its many virtues, the Equality Act 2010 can be seen as fulfilling this prediction; it consists of 218 sections and 28 schedules. The Act can be printed on 'just' 250 pages of A4 paper. The explanatory notes run to another 160 pages. Also associated with the Act are several hundred pages of various statutory codes of practice, as well as dozens of other, non-statutory guidance.

As for uncertainty; some of the most basic concepts in employment law – for example, when is a worker a contractor and when is she an employee? – have been subject to such repeated judicial comment, and such a wide variety of factors have been held to be potentially relevant, that it can feel as if a straightforward answer is no closer now than it was ten or twenty or even forty years ago.

A consistent feature of the common law over the past century and more has been the use (indeed over-use) of tests of 'reasonableness' which leave the widest possible margin to the Judge to rule on a case-by-case basis in whatever way that he or she might like. Such tests are prevalent throughout the common law, for example, in the tort of negligence, which requires a duty of care, which in turn is made out where there is a relationship of proximity between a respondent and a claimant, where it was *reasonably* foreseeable that negligence by the defendant would harm the claimant, and where it is fair, just and *reasonable* to impose a duty.[18]

There are very many reasonableness tests in contemporary employment law. To give a few examples: where a business transfer takes place, and an employer makes statements as to the likely impact on his employees, the employer must take *reasonable* care in making these statements.[19] A court, when deciding whether a dismissal was unfair, must ask itself whether the dismissal was within a band of *reasonable* responses, or, to put the matter only slightly differently, whether the dismissal was so bad that no *reasonable* employer would have done it.[20] If the reason for dismissal is misconduct, then there is a partial refinement of the test: a dismissal is unfair if there has been no *reasonable* investigation.[21] If a claimant has submitted a claim of unfair dismissal to a Tribunal more than three months after the date of termination, the Tribunal will have jurisdiction to hear the claim only where it was not *reasonably* practicable to submit the claim sooner.[22]

In pure legal theory, where a court is invited to apply a reasonableness test, it should do so by invoking an objective standard. That act is reasonable which would appear reasonable to a reasonable man – the average man, removed of all characteristics of age, class, race and so on (but, by tradition, not his gender). Critics have long been aware of the limitations of reasonableness. The reasonable man has been described as 'an odious and insufferable creature who never makes a mistake'.[23] The reasonable man is of course a fictional character, behind whose judgment stands the judgment of the Judge him- or herself.

Where so much depends on the Judge's opinion as to what constitutes a just conclusion, the claimed benefit of a system of case law based on precedent (that is, that the law is supposed to be predictable) is lost. Two cases on the same point and both by chance involving the same employer, illustrate the problem. As has been stated above, the basic rule when a claimant submits a claim of unfair dismissal to the Employment Tribunal late (that is, outside the initial three months of the facts giving rise to the case) is that the claim may only be heard when it was not 'reasonably practicable' for the claim to be submitted earlier. In 2005, the Royal Bank of Scotland (RBS) dismissed a Mr Theobald for gross misconduct. There was then an internal appeal. Mr Theobald took advice from a Citizens Advice Bureau, which advised him that he had to complete the internal appeal procedure before making an application to the Employment Tribunal. Mr Theobald ultimately learned that his internal appeal was unsuccessful at some point between 24 hours and 48 hours before the expiry of the three-month time limit. He then downloaded a Tribunal claim form. There were in effect either one or two days in which it was feasible for him to submit his form, before the time limits expired. Mr Theobald in fact submitted the form ten days later. On appeal, it was held that the claimant's failure to submit a form within this period of one or two days prevented the Tribunal from hearing the case.[24]

Fourteen months after Mr Theobald's case, Mr Bevan, another RBS employee, was also dismissed for gross misconduct. His internal appeal failed. He was sent the letter informing him that his appeal had been unsuccessful three days before the expiry of the three-month time limit and received the letter at home five hours before the deadline. In effect, Mr Bevan had just a few hours in which it was possible for him to submit his form, before the time limits expired. On appeal, it was held that it had not been practicable for Mr Bevan to submit the form in time, and accordingly the Tribunal agreed to extend its jurisdiction to hear the claim.[25]

It might be possible to distinguish these two cases by saying that as a rule of law where a claimant has 24 hours to complete a Tribunal form, it is reasonably practicable for them to do so, whereas when the claimant has five hours, it is not reasonably practicable. But if this was the law, the law would be unreasonably harsh. Mr Theobald had no prior experience of employment law. He was receiving advice from a Citizens Advice Bureau, but the CAB did not act as his representative, and even if it had been representing him, he would have had no real prospect of arranging a meeting with a CAB caseworker in the day or two that was available to him.

Reading between the lines, in *Theobald*, the EAT may have been influenced by a suspicion that the claimant was not telling the full truth about the vital 24- or 48-hour period. Equally, in *Bevan*, there is more than a hint that the Tribunal thought that the employer had kept its response to the claimant's internal appeal back to the last minute on purpose – to make life as difficult as possible for the claimant. But if these were the underlying considerations explaining the decisions, it can also be seen how very easily either case could have been decided differently.

THE COMMON LAW: A CULTURE ONLY PARTIALLY OPEN TO WORKERS' RIGHTS

There are other ways in which the legacy of the common law shapes the Employment Tribunal system. Common law logic is always backwards. It starts from previous legal decisions and asks what principles are compatible with a host of complex and contradictory previous cases. In such a system, there is always bound to be more at work than mere respect for the authority of past judgments. The judgments accumulate and a legal system starts to take on a settled character. At a level of very great abstraction, the common law is a tradition which:

1. tends to protect property rights in general, and
2. in particular encourages contractual disputes to be settled primarily on the basis of the terms actually contained within a contract (rather than by reference to say general values of fairness or justice), and
3. offers to the litigant in a civil dispute, or the defendant in a criminal case, a high level of fairness – in procedural terms.

The reason why precepts such as these dominate, even in courts such as Employment Tribunals, which were set up in the modern era, and are the product of statute rather than tradition, is that the lawyers who appear in the Employment Tribunal, their Judges, and the Judges who hear appeals from Tribunal cases, are all schooled in a common law tradition in which these values dominate.

As what is being discussed here is the entire legal system of the UK (as well as many former UK colonies), no amount of examples would be sufficient to prove that these trends are actually at work. But to give a few examples: (1) the 'common law's focus on the protection of property and contractual rights' (as it was described in 2011 by the Court of Appeal)[26] can be seen in the way that until the creation by Parliament of environmental standards over the past three decades, there was no common law right for a person to bring a claim for their own personal losses arising from environmental harm. The only equivalent right was a right of property-holders to bring claims in nuisance, that is, where their own personal right in a property was diminished by environmental harm.[27] Moreover, in nuisance, there has been a common law assumption that environmental damage was not actionable, where the property damaged was the property of the poor: 'What would be a nuisance in Belgrave Square would not necessarily be so in Bermondsey.'[28]

This chapter has already drawn attention to the very large number of ways that employment law relies on notions of reasonableness. The problem with this test, it has already said, is its subjectivity. Tests of reasonableness tend to make the law uncertain. We can go further: tests of reasonableness leave Judges a wide discretion to decide the law according to notions of what seems right to them in a given case. Where so much depends on the decision making of the individual, their personal background, character and tastes become over-important.

Our existing cadre of Employment Judges are overwhelmingly of a particular background: male, middle-aged, white, educated at public school and Oxbridge.[29] Now while this sort of training by no means guarantees that bad decisions will be made, it does undoubtedly train an individual towards certain notions of what constitutes reasonable behaviour when considering the conduct of any particular employee or employer. It encourages a general approach of deference towards existing property rights and towards the rights of both professionals and managers.

Along with reasonableness, another phrase which recurs in common law courts is common sense. For example, it is said to be 'common sense' that an employee's continuity of service is preserved where she takes a new job with a new employer that is bought by her old company after an employment interview, but before she starts work.[30] Where a Tribunal sends correspondence to the parties, it is deemed to be 'common sense' that the relevant date (for the purposes of deadlines in responding to the correspondence) is the date of postmark, not the date on the letter itself or the date of receipt.[31] The question of whether a claimant has been dismissed or resigned is to be decided by taking a 'practical and common sense' approach.[32] Even the question of when the reverse burden of proof applies in discrimination cases, has been said to be a matter of 'common sense'.[33]

Many years ago, the Italian philosopher Antonio Gramsci observed that common sense is an ideologically loaded way of looking at the world, which tends to leave property and social relationships intact.[34] In the common law, however, it is exactly this very same common-sense reasoning which is constantly encouraged.

Further, as regards (2), the presumption that the courts should never disregard the express words of a contract, even where (for example) the contract has been written by one party only with the other party being in a subordinate position,[35] has been repeatedly affirmed, and was given a judicial gloss by Lord Jessel, in the case of *Printing and Numerical Registering Co* v *Sampson*, when he ruled 'Contracts when entered into voluntarily shall be held *sacred*' (emphasis added).[36]

The main approach of the common law is to read contracts carefully, closely, and only look with extreme reluctance outside the contract for a reason to disregard any term. This is not just a matter of employment law, but the starting approach of the common law to all different sorts of contractual disputes. In 2003, for example, it was stated by Lord Hobhouse in the House of Lords that in an ordinary contractual dispute, there is not merely a rule of law that the terms of the contract will defeat evidence that the parties intended to make an agreement in different terms, there is in addition a rule of evidence that information which might contradict the express wording of the contract *is not even allowed to be put before the court*:

> The rule that other evidence may not be adduced to contradict the provisions of a contract contained in a written document is fundamental to the mercantile law of this country; the bargain is the document; the certainty of the contract depends on it ... When the parties have deliberately put their agreement into writing, it is conclusively presumed ... that they intend the writing to form a full and final statement of their intentions, and one which should be placed beyond the reach of future controversy, bad faith or treacherous memory ... This rule is one of the great strengths of English commercial law and is one of the main reasons for the international success of English law in preference to laxer systems which do not provide the same certainty.[37]

While this rule of evidence would not apply at the Tribunal,[38] the underlying policy presumption that the good functioning of a commercial society depends on reading contracts literally is shared by Employment Judges. For workers, the vast majority of whom of course have no power to negotiate the terms of their employment contract, but who are required to work on standard-terms contracts, this creates a constant disadvantage. Should a contract, for example, enable an employer to require a worker to work (on instruction) at a town anywhere in England, the worker will get little satisfaction from the court if she claims later that the term was unreasonable. There is a standard judicial answer: 'you signed the contract, didn't you?'[39] There is no overriding rule that employers are required to treat employees fairly.[40] They are required to treat them only as well as the contract requires.

As to (3), this is the best face of the common law – the tradition of jury trial, the right to remain silent, and the assumption of innocence for defendants. One reason why there has been such an extraordinary rewriting of the criminal law in the past 15 years is because the common law (with historically several false starts[41]) has come to offer defendants a high standard of procedural fairness. In an era of terrorism trials, these standards act as a rebuke to Tory and New Labour politicians alike.

One guide to the employment courts, published in 1973, emphasised that Tribunal justice was about good procedure as much as good outcomes:

> A Tribunal's job is only partly done when it has obtained the 'right' answer to a question before it. Another, perhaps major, part of its job is to ensure that, as far as is practicable, both parties, the one who lost as well as the one who won, are satisfied that the answer is indeed the 'right' one.[42]

An Employment Judge writing today, nearly four decades later, would no doubt endorse these remarks. The origin of this emphasis on procedural justice is the common law. A legal system which tried to treat criminal defendants fairly extends the same courtesy to employment claimants.

Yet, as has been emphasised throughout this chapter, procedural justice does not always produce substantive justice. While the common law gives claimants certain rights, there are other rights which it takes away.

The ongoing force of the common law acts as a continuing obstacle to reform, so that any future and genuinely reform-minded government would also discover that many of the worst barriers for claimants are the product of common law Judges, and in these terms barely capable of repeal. For example, as we saw in a previous chapter, the rule that agency workers should not be able to succeed in unfair dismissal claims was the product of a decision of the EAT in *James* v *Greenwich Council*, as recently as 2006. The court justified its decision by reference to common law principles, including the need to respect the written contracts which deprived agency workers of employee status:

> We should not leave this case without repeating the observations made by many courts in the past that many agency workers are highly vulnerable and need to be protected from the abuse of economic power by the end users. *The common law can only tinker with the problem on the margins.*[43]

Were Parliament to pass legislation that, in future, agency workers should be assumed to be employees, the Judges would have difficulty in escaping their common law training, with its emphasis on the words of contracts and would still feel a pressure to find that many or most agency workers were not employees.

Other possible reforms, whether to enable claims for reinstatement or to increase the amount of compensation for unfair dismissal, could face similar problems. The poor results achieved by many workers are not mainly the fault of hostile statutory schemes (even if flaws can be identified in the various Acts), but are just as much the consequence of judge-made law.

9
Employment Tribunals in Crisis?

There are some people for whom the prospect of litigation, of 'appearing in court', holds no terrors. The average Englishman, and in particular the average English employee, is not one of these people: if the pursuit of his legal rights involves an appearance in the court, it is quite likely that he will forego his rights rather than take those distasteful steps.[1]

The Government looks likely to be inundated with Employment Tribunal applications this year as firms continue to slash jobs at a record pace.[2]

For much of the past decade, the press coverage of Tribunals has been dominated by concerns about the increasing numbers of claims. Sometimes the number of claims is set to be 'rising', sometimes it is 'soaring'.[3] The one story that never seems to be reported is that in any one year the number of Tribunal claims has fallen; which it did for example in 2002–03, in 2004–05, in 2008–09 and 2010–11. It is true, of course, that the pattern has indeed been one of a general increase in Tribunal claims over many years. What is more galling is to see, overlaid onto this reality, press stories using a rising number of Tribunal claims to push notions (often culled from poorly referenced business sources) that claimants are greedy and their claims fanciful.

In 2004, for example, the *Independent* reported a CBI survey which claimed that more than two-thirds of employers were reporting a rise in 'dubious, weak and vexatious' claims.[4] These figures sound awfully definite, until one remembers that that there are roughly 2.1 million employers in the country.[5] Since there were around 90,000 Tribunal claims in 2004, by definition at least nineteen-twentieths of all businesses saw no Tribunal claims at all. Who then were the 'two-thirds' of businesses reporting an increase in claims? And how were these supposedly 'vexatious' claims supposed to be distinguished from non-vexatious claims?

Beginning with the recession that began in 2008, the press has been full of stories predicting that the number of Tribunal claims would rise.[6] Perhaps the most extraordinary take on the story was the press attempts to join the twin pandemics of increasing Tribunal claims and swine flu. Newspapers warned that employees exposed to the H1N1 virus at work would no doubt bring claims to the Tribunal. Employers were warned to expect in particular Tribunal claims for 'personal injury' and 'health and safety',[7] cases which, of course, the Tribunal would have had no jurisdiction to hear.

It was simple common sense that the number of redundancy dismissals was going to rise during the recession, and therefore at least one category of claims (unfair dismissals) was likely to increase in turn. There was little consideration, however, of the possibility that the total number of claims might fall – for example, because potential claimants who remained in employment were afraid of victimisation and dismissal if they did bring claims. Yet between 2007–08 and 2008–09, the total number of Tribunal claims did fall. Increases in the number of redundancy pay, breach of contract and unfair dismissal claims (up 48 per cent, 31 per cent and 29 per cent respectively) were more than offset by decreases in the (larger) number of sex discrimination and equal pay cases (down 31 and 27 per cent respectively).[8]

Faced with figures that were falling (when the press had predicted that they would rise), reporters settled on the expedient of selecting *only* those that were rising, to give a false impression that the general rise they had predicted had in fact occurred. 'Unfair dismissal and redundancy tribunal claims rocket', claimed one report; 'Unfair dismissal claims rise by almost a third since 2008', said another.[9]

More Tribunals, it is always said, means more costs for employers. But even if so, we still need to ask *how much?* In 2008, one business website estimated the cost of Tribunals to business as £200 million per year (or about £2,700 per case that made it to the Tribunal stage). This relatively plausible figure was soon to be supplanted in the press coverage by other, wilder estimates. In September 2009, the Forum of Private Business (FPB) announced the results of a survey suggesting that the costs to business of employment law compliance stood at around twelve times more, or £2.4 billion per year.[10] (If this was true, it would be about 20 per cent more than the government spends each year on all civil and criminal legal aid combined.)[11] Not to be outdone, the CBI then claimed that the true cost to business of changes to employment law since 1998 has been a staggering £73 billion,[12] or more than £2,500 for every worker in the UK workforce. The method of this estimate was to use the government's own costs for the introduction of new employment-related Acts or Regulations since 1998, multiplying this cost by each year in which the Regulation had been in force, and then adding together the figures for each different piece of legislation. If the figures were not high enough, they were simply increased a little further, to generate a larger overall headline figure. In this way, the cost of the Sex Discrimination Act 1975 (Amendment) Regulations 2008 was estimated by the CBI to be an extraordinary £497 million.[13] Lest readers feel overwhelmed by the extravagance of government waste on this scale, it should be recalled that the primary purposes of these Regulations were as follows:

1. To amend a poorly composed section of previous Regulations which appeared to require pregnant women bringing discrimination claims to name a comparator (prior to the previous Regulations, women did not need to so this; and after the publication of the final Regulations they did not – in other words, the actual law was never changed at all); and
2. To extend the statutory wording where women brought claims of sex harassment; to widen this slightly from cases where harassment was on 'on the ground of' a woman's sex, to cases 'related to her sex or that of another person'.

Civil servants' estimate of the total costs of these Regulations to business was £15 million in the first year (that is, 2008–09) and £250,000 per annum thereafter;[14] and even these figures are implausibly high. How the CBI report could stretch this figure from £15 million to £497 million by autumn 2009 is not clear from their survey.

It would be wrong to fix on this one survey as being particularly bad. It is better seen as being indicative of a whole school of corporate PR in which junk statistics are developed, repeated without care, and then further magnified in press reporting. The method is pervasive. Trying to estimate the average costs to an employer of defending an ordinary Employment Tribunal claim in 2010, the British Chambers of Commerce came up with the figure of £125,000. Those bothering to read the report's footnotes would have found that this figure was based on the best guess of one HR manager at a single corporate firm.[15] Three years earlier, the Department of Trade and Industry had published a rather more plausible estimate of £9,000.[16]

'REFORM': MARK I

Twice in the last decade of the Labour government, legislation was introduced to reduce the number of Tribunal cases; on neither occasion did it prove a success. In 2002, Parliament passed an Employment Act, which among other changes introduced compulsory grievance and dismissal procedures. Where an employer sought to discipline or dismiss a worker, the employer would be required to send a letter to the employee inviting them to a meeting and giving them reasons for the meeting. Where the meeting might result in dismissal, the employer was obliged to set out this possibility in their letter. After the meeting, the employer had to inform the employee of the outcome of the meeting. The employee had a right of appeal against the employer's decision. Where an employee had a complaint against an employer, the employee was required to follow a parallel process, making a complaint in writing, leading to a grievance hearing with a right of appeal.

The most complex parts of the new model concerned the relationship between these internal procedures and any subsequent Tribunal claim. In effect, there were three scenarios. First, if the employee's complaint concerned dismissal, then the employee was not required to appeal the dismissal before submitting a Tribunal claim. It was, however, sensible to appeal, as any ultimate reward could be reduced by between 10 and 50 per cent for the employee's failure to follow the procedures.

Secondly, where the employee's complaint concerned a matter other than dismissal, the employee was required to put in a grievance before bringing a Tribunal claim. A failure to raise a grievance meant no claim would be heard. Claims could be submitted not less than 28 days after a grievance. Where a grievance had been submitted and the employee reasonably believed it was still live three months later, the time limit for submitting a claim would be extended to six months.

Third, the scenario frequently arose that the same act required both an appeal and a grievance. This would happen if, for example, a dismissal had been done on discriminatory grounds. In these circumstances, the claimant would be advised to follow both the above routes at once, submitting two claims forms at different times and applying to join them, plus in all probability having to endure some preliminary arguments from the employer that either or both claims were timed out.

These rules came into effect on 1 October 2004.[17] Horribly complex as the new statutory process was, the ostensible logic of the process was straightforward. If a worker was required to make a complaint, before proceeding, and the case was weak, she would soon realise this by the way in which the employer rejected their complaint. If the case was strong, the employer would accept it, resolving the dispute without any need for the courts to get involved.

The Regulations were complex, and there was pressure before their introduction from trade unions, ACAS and other bodies for the procedures to be simplified or withdrawn. This demand was resisted. Civil servants estimated that the procedures would result in a net reduction of Tribunal cases amounting to 34,000–37,000 cases per year,[18] thereby saving both employers and government. The introduction of the procedures thus formed part of that trend in general towards the idealisation of 'entrepreneurial prosperity', which even sympathetic authors perceived to be a defining goal of our last government.[19]

One problem with the Regulations was that they put too much onus on managers within companies to deal fairly with workers' complaints and to uphold them where they were merited. An earlier chapter of this book showed that, in the 1960s, workers' appeals against dismissal in different industries had a success rate of very roughly between a third and a fifth. I know of no similar studies today, but if there were any I doubt they would find that the claimant's success rate in overturning dismissals by appeals or grievances was as high as 5 per cent. Employers, and society in general, have different expectations of managers. In the most general terms, 40 years ago, most workplaces had at least some independent-minded managers, who were zealous to protect their own sections, if need be, from the whims of senior management. Since then, the phenomenon of the independent-minded manager has become so rare as to be practically extinct. Ideas of management have been imported from the US, and popularised through television. A manager today protecting his or her workers from unfair dismissal would be seen as disloyal. The manager too would be marked down to be sacked in due course.

The procedures did lead to a one-off reduction in the number of cases, which fell from 115,042 in 2003–04 to 86,189 in 2004–05. In the following years, however, the number of cases began to rise again. Some of the rise since may be explained by extraneous factors that would have been difficult to predict in 2002 or 2004. For example, there was a sharp rise in the number of equal pay claims, from 4,159 in 2003–04 to 62,706 in 2007–08,[20] with the main explanation (as we have seen) being the national single-status agreement in local government, which employers were required to implement locally by 2007. Looking back on this period as a whole, it may well be that the dispute resolution procedures were in fact successful on their own terms, and that they reduced the number of Tribunal claims, even to the extent that the government had hoped. Yet the fall was offset by other facts causing the total number of claims to rise, and measures introduced to reduce the number of Tribunal claims turned out to be more costly in other ways than had been expected.

'REFORM': MARK II

In December 2006, some two years or so after the statutory dispute resolutions came into effect, the Department of Trade and Industry invited Michael Gibbons, previously the director of UK Communications at PowerGen, to oversee a review of employment dispute resolution in Britain. The report was published in March 2007. Its proposals were endorsed (if obliquely) by then Chancellor of the Exchequer Gordon Brown in his final, triumphant budget speech.[21] The report informed an Employment Simplification Bill, which received royal assent as the Employment Act 2008. Michael Gibbons' report brimmed with the confidence of a senior executive who expected his instructions to be implemented by his juniors without question or delay:

> I present a suite of complementary recommendations which, in aggregate, are genuinely deregulatory, and simplifying ... If implemented, they should reduce the complexity of the current system and reduce costs to businesses and employees ... I believe they should be cost effective for Government to implement.[22]

Three issues dominated the Gibbons report. The first was simply the cost of the Employment Tribunals, which Gibbons estimated was £120 million per year.[23] The second issue was the number of cases going to Tribunal, which the report was designed to reduce. The report's main proposal – the repeal of the statutory dispute resolution procedures introduced in 2004 – was justified as a step to reduce the number of cases and hence the cost of the system. The third idea was that employment law had been allowed to become over-complex and required simplification. These criticisms were presented as the common concern of experts drawn from every sphere of industry. The report was welcomed by both the TUC and the CBI. Its findings became the common policy ambition of both the Labour and Conservative parties, and of the majority of newspaper columnists to consider the issue. Yet the unanimity with which

Gibbons' proposals were welcomed should not conceal the extent to which they meshed analyses that pointed in different directions. The Tribunal is an adversarial system. The majority of claimants have certain common experiences, which are different from those of their employers. Any single set of 'reforms' will always affect the parties differently.

Gibbons complained that too many cases were brought each year. Between 1 January and 31 December 1972, for example, some 13,555 cases came to the Tribunal, while between 1 April 2010 and 31 March 2011, there were 218,100, a sixteen-fold rise. Indeed, much of the growth has taken place after the introduction of the statutory dispute resolution procedures in 2004. They do appear to have achieved a one-off reduction in the Tribunal workload; the problem for government was that this was followed by several years in which the number of claims rose (see Table 9.1).

Table 9.1 Employment Tribunal applications (select years)[24]

April 2003–March 2004	115,042
April 2004–March 2005	86,189
April 2005–March 2006	115,039
April 2006–March 2007	132,577
April 2007–March 2008	189,303
April 2008–March 2009	151,028
April 2009–March 2010	236,100
April 2010–March 2011	218,100

To put these figures in context: in 1985, there were 25.3 million workers in the UK. Just over 1 in 100 of all workers were dismissed at some point in that year. In 1985, there were 33,000 Tribunal applications complaining of unfair dismissal. In short, roughly one in eight of all dismissed workers used the Tribunals to gain a remedy.[25] Another survey has estimated that around one in 20 of all workers (5.8 per cent) who experience problems with their rights at work will end up bringing a Tribunal claim.[26] Since 1985, the total number of dismissals in the economy each year has almost certainly risen, but even today, at around 220,000 claims from a workforce of around 30 million, the total number of claims each year is still only one for every 130 workers. By contrast, a 2006 ACAS report estimated that the total number of claimants bringing claims each year in France was 0.7 per cent of the workforce (or one in every 140 workers), and in Germany 1.5 per cent (the equivalent of one in 60 workers).[27]

Gibbons suggested not just that there were too many cases in general, but that there were too many weak and vexatious cases in particular. Indeed, many employers have since Gibbons complained that workers see Tribunals as a sort of low-odds, high-payout lottery, an additional payment to be granted to dismissed former workers whether or not their claim is merited. Claimants are sometimes termed 'have-a-go-heroes',[28] well-off former workers, protected against detriment in their new position, people who can express a wholly unfounded grievance without sanction in their new post. But this image is a myth; after all, if we count only claims which make it to a hearing, *three-fifths of Tribunal claimants win*.

The correct criticism of the statutory dispute resolution procedures would have been that they brought lawyers into employment relationships, prematurely and unhappily. This was indeed a complaint of employers, that under the new procedures workers approached lawyers earlier. Even simple procedural steps, such as a worker's submission of a letter or grievance became subject to complex legal advice, with solicitors treating this stage as if it was the equivalent to the submission of particulars of claim in the civil courts. Workers were warned that by failing to raise their full claim at this stage, they might be prevented from bringing a matter to the Tribunal later. Employers, finding properly drafted legal letters at this very early stage, responded in kind, taking legal advice, which usually went to the best way to dismiss a worker rather than whether dismissal was the right answer: 'As anyone who has had to deal with [the procedures] can testify, they are bureaucratic, onerous and almost impossible to follow in places. What was intended to spare parties the legal costs of a Tribunal process instead just 'front loaded' those costs.'[29]

Reform took the form of an Employment Act 2008, repealing the 2004 procedures, which were replaced by the old pre-2004 law plus a new ACAS code.[30] Breaches of the code can now result in an increase or a reduction in damages, but the maximum up- or down-lift is only 25 per cent, and the content of the code is considerably less prescriptive than the statutory dispute resolution procedures it replaced. The 2008 Act did nothing to prevent vexatious claims; and by reducing the requirement to submit a grievance before bringing a Tribunal claim, it actually made it slightly easier for workers to issue a claim. This is part of the reason why the number of claims then rose: the Gibbons report had the opposite effect to the one intended.

The lasting significance of the Gibbons report is that it encouraged a number of employers and business-friendly journalists to begin a complaint which had not been heard for several years, namely that the Tribunal system was broken and in need of dramatic change. The Engineering Employers' Federation asked if Tribunals remained 'fit for purpose'.[31] The *Financial Times* went further, calling on the government to deliver employers from a system like 'Dante's vision of the Inferno'.[32]

The Labour government encouraged businesses to think that Tribunals were in need of major change. In repealing legislation which was intended to reduce the number of employment claims, and which was partially successful on these terms, but replacing it with new laws which did nothing to reduce the number of Tribunal claims, it raised employer's expectations, without doing anything to satisfy them. The real and evident danger was that employers would return asking for 'more'.

'REFORM': MARK III

After selecting David Cameron as their new leader in December 2005, the Conservatives were initially determined to shed their image as 'the nasty party'. In the employment sphere, this required them to promote policies that would put burdens on business. In 2007, for example, Theresa May announced a series of measures to promote equal pay, the centrepiece of which was the proposal that an employer found guilty of discrimination by a Tribunal would be required in consequence to undergo a compulsory gender pay audit.[33] As the 2010 general election approached, however, the party's message changed, and the desire to promote any bona fide reforms weakened. There was a sole reference to Tribunals in the Tories' election Manifesto: 'We will review employment and workplace laws, for employers and employees, to ensure they maximise flexibility for both parties while protecting fairness.'[34] It appeared that the Conservatives' prime target was health and safety, where the ground had been softened by a long-standing tabloid campaign.

By the winter of 2010–11, it was slowly becoming clear that the new government did have various 'big ideas' to change the Tribunal system. The government's then 'enterprise tsar' Lord Young initially proposed, during an interview on Radio 4's *Today* programme, that the qualifying period for unfair dismissal should be doubled from one year's continuous service to two. There was then a proposal, leaked to the *Telegraph* that workers should have to pay an issuing fee for starting a claim.

In the press, a number of industry voices were recruited to act as cheerleaders for these measures, including Helen Giles, the human resources director of the Broadway housing charity. Giles told *The Times* in January 2011 that the Labour government had not reviewed the Employment Tribunal system (untrue), that employers were deliberately recruiting illegal immigrants in order to circumvent employment laws (if so, their conduct would be a criminal offence),[35] that the workers lost the 'majority of cases' (again untrue), and that employees only brought their claims because of claimant lawyers, who she described as 'parasitical creatures'.[36] This was then followed up by a second *Times* piece, in which Giles opened with the robust-sounding statistic that three out of five employers had been subject to a race or sex discrimination claim.[37] Given that there are 20,000 such claims a year,[38] and that there are over 2 million employers in the country,[39] the accurate figure is that no more than 1.05 per cent of employers a year is subject to such a claim.

Eventually, at the end of January 2011, the government began a formal consultation on what was a combined package of measures to redraw the Tribunal system. This contained a total of 13 linked 'reforms':

1) Require all claims to be submitted to Acas in the first instance to offer pre-claim conciliation,
2) Stronger case management powers for weak and unmeritorious cases,
3) Provision of information,
4) Formalise offers to settle,
5) Witness statements to be taken as read,
6) Withdraw payment of expenses for employment tribunals,
7) Extend the jurisdictions where judges can sit alone,
8) Introduce the use of legal officers,
9) Elaborate the overriding objective,
10) Introduce fee charging,
11) Increase qualification periods for unfair dismissal,
12) Introduce financial penalties for employers and
13) Review calculation of limits for employment tribunal awards and redundancy.[40]

By far the most significant measures within this list were proposals 10 and 11, the introduction of fee charging, and the increased qualification requirement for unfair dismissal claims.

At present, an employee is required to have been in continuous employment for 12 months to bring an unfair dismissal claim; the government now proposes to increase this to two years. This would disadvantage the one in eight workers who at any time have more than a year but less than two years' service.[41] It would not improve access to justice; it would simply reduce the rights of vulnerable workers.

When the Tribunal system was first established, the qualification period for unfair dismissal was six months. This was increased twice under the Conservative governments of the 1980s before being reduced to its present figure (12 months) in 1999, partly in response to a decision of the House of Lords in *R* v *Secretary of State for Employment, ex p Seymour-Smith* that a two-year qualifying period indirectly discriminated against women who were less likely to have accrued lengthy service.[42]

Supporters of a longer qualifying period could argue that in the ten years since the rules were changed (that is, 1999–2009), the number of Tribunal cases increased by 64 per cent. More cases have come to the Tribunal, causing the taxpayer expense. Against that it must be noted that in the preceding ten years (1989–99), the number of Tribunal cases had grown by 210 per cent,[43] suggesting that the processes driving the increasing use of litigation by workers go deeper than this tweaking of the rules.

This book has argued that the reason why there are now so many Tribunal claims is that litigation fills a space left by the partial decline of industrial bargaining, and by the decreasing independence of workplace dispute resolution procedures, so that someone who has a genuine grievance about their work increasingly has no option but to sue. That need will continue, whatever the qualification period.

As for the issuing fee, the injustice of the proposal is shown by the suggestion that workers should pay a fee but employers should not have to pay a fee to defend the claim. The case in favour of requiring claimants only to pay a fee is essentially Gibbons' argument,[44] that Tribunals are dominated by unmerited complaints. But as we have seen, this is hardly borne out by the evidence that at most hearings claimants succeed. If Tribunal time is wasted, there is a better case to say that the primary culprits are employers running hopeless defences to reasonable claims.

In a speech to the 2011 Conservative Party Conference Chancellor George Osborne proposed setting the total amount of the Tribunal hearing and issuing fee at £1250; at this level, it would be a punitive tax on vulnerable workers.

Neither proposal was intended to protect fairness. This can be seen by the content of the proposals. Each is a restrictive mechanism directed at claimants. But a Tribunal claim is a series of alternate steps involving first the claimant and then the respondent. If it was thought that there were too many hearings, it would be possible to reduce both the total number of claims and also the total number of responses.

There are lots of different ways in which weak responses could be restricted. We have seen in earlier chapters for example that in the large majority of wages claims the claimant succeeds. An employer could be required, in such cases, under the threat of having the claim granted without a hearing, to specify the payments that had been made to the employee, the dates on which they were made, and the reason why the employer believed that there were no further sums owed to the claimant. Changes could equally be made to the Tribunal rules, to require a response to be struck out unless returned within 28 days of receipt of the claimant's claim form (rather than as present, where the time limits are applied strictly against claimants, but with the greatest possible flexibility in favour of respondents).[45]

The drafters of the consultation document could clearly see the difficulty of introducing one-sided measures which would make life more difficult for workers and easier for employers.[46] Yet rather than implement mirrored proposals having an effect on both sides, they settled on offering workers the alternative suggestion that for certain categories of workplace dispute, employers who breached the law should have to pay a penalty, not to the claimant, but to the government (proposal 12 in the list above). The weakness of this proposal is that it would rely on claimants to bring claims against employers, while giving no incentive for them to do so. Moreover, the consultation document contained no thought-through proposals to explain which breaches of what laws, and what kinds of breach, would carry penalties.

The other proposals can be dealt with more briefly. Requiring all claims to be submitted to ACAS in the first instance would delay the hearing, and therefore the conclusion of claims. It would entrench the parties, making later settlement less likely. By introducing an intermediary stage before the hearing of the case, it would risk duplicating the faults of the previous dispute resolution procedure.

Moreover, the government's proposal would also change ACAS's relationship to the parties. At present, ACAS's role is to provide an independent voice facilitating settlement where so required. It is a mediator not an adviser. The suggestion is that in future,

ACAS officers, who have had no legal training, should be able to advise parties on their rights as a prelude to settlement. As, in practice, employers already have access to legal advice, in reality, the proposal is that ACAS should direct claimants to settle, relying on the ACAS officer's understanding of the law. Now some ACAS officers already display a tendency towards 'mission creep'. Because it is their job to encourage settlement, and because in a settlement dialogue a side with representation will naturally be better placed to make its settlement arguments sound more legally robust than one without, a definite minority of ACAS officers engage in settlement discussions by simply repeating whatever the employer's solicitor says, but with more effect (as they, unlike the employer's solicitor, are seen as independent). Surveys of claimants disclose complaints about ACAS:[47]

> [The ACAS representative] was a complete and utter waste of space. He actually upset me ... I was never asking him to make decisions, because he can't do that. But you know, he also is not supposed to take a side and I didn't always necessarily believe what he said to me either. You know what, this is really awful, but I didn't trust him ... I was really, really disappointed.

Indeed the current evidence is that the more contact a claimant had had with a named ACAS officer, the less satisfied they will be about the outcome of their case.[48]

Of course, conciliation could be an alternative to litigation, and there are other areas of law (for example, family disputes about contact with children) where an emphasis on settlement, and the active supervision of both the courts and the children's guardian's service Cafcass, tends to protect the interests of all the parties. But the key to making conciliation work is to provide venues, people and resources; rather than compulsory conversations down a telephone to a conciliator trying to force through a settlement.

By stronger case management powers for weak and unmeritorious cases, the government means that Tribunals should have additional powers to limit workers' abilities to bring claims, and in particular to require claimants to pay deposits of up to £1,000 (the current figure is £500). Yet it was not proposed that the test should be altered as to when such deposits should be required, and the practice has been that such deposits are only required in unusual cases. The government proposes in addition that an Employment Judge should have the power to strike out claims at a case management discussion as well as at a pre-hearing review. This proposal is likely to be opposed by the Appellate Judges who repeatedly complain that Judges strike out meritorious claims prematurely, compelling the appeal courts to send claims – after a long delay – back to the beginning to be heard properly.[49]

By provision of information, the government intended that respondents should be empowered to ask tribunals to order claimants to produce additional details of their claim. This duplicates powers the Tribunal has already.

The government proposed to increase the maximum Tribunal costs award from £10,000 to £20,000. The injustice of this proposal can be considered by considering the typical resources of the average worker and the average employer. A £20,000 costs award is equivalent to more than four-fifths of the average salary; to most large companies it is not the least drop in the ocean.

The next proposal was that witness statements should be read in future by the Tribunal, rather than aloud by the witness (as had been the normal practice in the Tribunal in the past). This will do very little to alter the balance between respondent and claimant, and was in any event established as best practice from the winter of 2010.[50]

Withdrawing payment of expenses for Employment Tribunals would be a small but definite inconvenience for those claimants, claimants' witnesses, and interpreters who have their travel and accommodation paid to attend a Tribunal hearing.

The consultation document proposed to extend the jurisdictions where Employment Judges could sit alone, from money claims (where it is already commonplace) to unfair dismissal, albeit not to discrimination cases. Again, this would be a retrograde step, tending to increase the sense that employment law is a matter for trained lawyers (Judges) rather than the lay Tribunal members.

At present, all case management decisions are made by Employment Judges. The government's proposal was that some of this could be passed on to a more junior category of lawyer, 'legal officers'. This should not be objectionable, so long as there were clear (and publicly accessible guidelines) as to what sort of case would be passed down in this way, and so long as the fully qualified Judges retained some power of review of case management decisions taken at this level.

The proposal to elaborate the overriding objective would mean in practice that when reaching case management decisions, the Tribunal should allot to each case 'an appropriate share of the Tribunal's resources, while taking into account the need to allot resources to other cases.' This provision is modelled on a provision in the civil court procedure, where it does little discernible harm (but equally no good).

Finally, the government's proposals to reviewing the limits for Tribunal awards was not intended to match the awards to workers' actual losses following dismissal. Instead, it was proposed that if such awards are uplifted in future it should be by the Consumer Prices Index, rather than the Retail Prices Index, as is done at present. The former is the government's preferred measure of inflation, as it excludes mortgage costs, and therefore usually produces a lower figure.

The government's estimate of the net effect of these measures was that they would result in an annual transfer of wealth from workers to their employers of £88.5 million a year,[51] which figure is in all likelihood a gross underestimate.[52]

Moreover, these proposals were not the only measures being canvassed by government which would impact negatively on Tribunal claimants. At the same time, the government was consulting on proposed changes to legal aid, which would remove access to legal help for claimants in wages and dismissal cases,[53] and introduce new means tests which were intended to reduce the number of workers able to claim legal aid. The government even had plans for a new referral system under which claimants would not be allowed to approach solicitors directly, but would first have to phone a central telephone bank staffed by non-lawyers, and gain authorisation from that source before being able to contact a legal aid lawyer. The government envisaged the total civil legal aid bill would be reduced by 42 per cent,[54] the majority of these savings being achieved by a brute reduction in the number of claimants getting any access at all to legal aid. One body which commented on the legal aid proposals was the Judges' Council of England and Wales:

> A notable achievement of the legal aid system has been the embedding of Legal Help in community advice work and the development of advice agencies with a local reputation for being helpful and someone you can trust. They are generally run efficiently and comparatively cheaply. They realise that not every problem needs a lawyer, but they are the doorway through which the disadvantaged can learn of the possibility of a legal solution to their problems in an appropriate case ... We fear that the effect of the withdrawal of Legal Help will be to make many of these agencies unsustainable. It is difficult to see what alternative

> sources of funding will be available to them, especially at a time of severe cut-backs in local authority expenditure.[55]

This has not been the only judicial intervention in response to the present programme of cuts. In *Gayle* v *Sandwell*, a decision of the Court of Appeal in July 2011, Lord Justice Mummery criticised the tendency of the press and politicians to over-emphasise the costs of Tribunals to the state and to business:

> As for those who complain about the time taken and the legal costs and other expenses and losses incurred, I think that they would want the hearings to be conducted in the interests of justice to both sides. I have seen very few constructive suggestions for practical improvements. If workers are given rights, there must be properly qualified, impartial and independent tribunals to adjudicate on them in accordance with a fair procedure. If workers are not given the necessary means for the just adjudication of their claims, procedures of a more rough and ready non-judicial kind may be used. The alternative procedures would probably not be impartial, independent or just, and are unlikely to do much for public order, social harmony or national prosperity.[56]

The challenge is to propose reforms that would improve the system without reverting to the rough-and-ready employer's justice that Mummery rightly decried.

Conclusion: How Could Tribunals be Reformed?

I stay, delay and put off judgment, so that the suit, well-ventilated, scrutinised, and batted around, may be borne more easily by the losing parties.[1]

The one great principle of the English law is to make business for itself. There is no other principle distinctly, certainly, and consistently maintained through all its narrow turnings.[2]

In the last chapter, I have described some recent changes to Tribunal procedure as well as the Coalition government's current malign proposals for 'reform'. It follows that there must be equivalent proposals, which would have more benign content. Through this book, I have argued that there are various dynamics which guide Tribunals to certain results. One is the legacy of decisions made by the Donovan Commission, and enacted in the Industrial Relations Act 1971, including (a) the decision to extend the power to hear cases of unfair dismissals to the existing Industrial Tribunals, and (b) the decision that the ordinary consequence of a finding of unfair dismissal would be an award of compensation rather than reinstatement.

REFORM 1: INSISTING ON REINSTATEMENT

From the second of these processes, it follows that one reform which would beneficially alter the relationship between workers and the Employment Tribunal would be to make reinstatement the primary remedy for unfair dismissal.[3] This could be done by amending section 112 of the Employment Rights Act 1996 so that the remedy for unfair dismissal would be the reinstatement of the complainant; with the claimant only (and not the employer) having the right to seek compensation instead.

The key justification for making reinstatement the primary remedy in unfair dismissal cases is that it would diminish the opportunity for poor management to ruin workers' lives. Anyone who has acted for workers in more than a handful of employment cases will know that Employment Tribunals are littered with daily instances of practices such as employers dismissing employees on false charges of misconduct, or raising allegations of incapability as a stratagem to avoid paying what (for workers with lengthy periods of continuous service) may be relatively generous contractual redundancy payments, or dismissing following serious allegations which the employer has never bothered to properly investigate.

A worker who loses a secure post and cannot be reinstated will, of necessity, have to find new employment in a hostile job market. She loses her ties to a job in which she may well have been successful and content.

Now, if reinstatement was to become the primary remedy for unfair dismissal, this could only be achieved *and work* if the time between the issuing of a claim form and the proceedings were dramatically reduced. At present, it is by no means unusual for nine months or even a year to be lost between the submitting of the ET1 form and the full merits hearing. It is hardly unusual for an employee to be dismissed on a marginal decision (while retaining supporters among some fellow workers in the dismissing company), and then for the parties' representatives to be engaged in several months of increasingly heated correspondence. This is then followed by a contested hearing, with the eventual result that not merely does the employer never want to see the claimant again, the claimant herself is equally embittered and has no great desire to be re-engaged. Prospects of achieving reinstatement, either by settlement, or by Tribunal order, would be dramatically increased if Tribunals were heard within a few weeks rather than months or years of the original decision to dismiss.

The law already contains (albeit rarely used) provisions to deal with circumstances where workers' representatives[4] are dismissed and can show a prime facie case of unfair dismissal. In these circumstances, the representative may make an application to the Tribunal within seven days of dismissal for interim reinstatement. The Tribunal must then determine the application 'as soon as practicable'.[5] The statute suggests a response of urgency to dismissals. At least in principal, this speed of response should not be the sole preserve of workers' representatives but should be available to all dismissed workers.

REFORM 2: BRING FORWARD THE LAY PANEL

There is no good reason why cases should take a year from issuing to hearing. Delay saves the system no money, the same cases still require to be heard, and the same total costs are incurred by the taxpayer. It may be that one reason that the time between issuing and hearing has extended is the lack of availability of sufficient numbers of Employment Judges. If so, this in turn begs the question of whether the Tribunal could be reconstituted in future, perhaps (as in France) as four-person panels, to include two people having an interest in employment relations from the employer's perspective and two people having an interest from the employee's perspective, but no Judge. If this was adopted, any decisions would of course have to be made by consensus. Yet consensus decision making is realistic: even in the present system, the number of cases where 'employer' and 'employee' members come to a different decision is very few. There are already many hundreds of Tribunal members who are well-used to reaching decisions in employment cases. They could be retained as the first members of a reformed Tribunal system. Employment Judges could be kept in reserve for appeals. Or there could be a legal adviser assisting the Tribunals on points of law (as happens in the Magistrates' courts).

In the absence of a lawyer chairing the Tribunal panel, it is most likely that the trend in the new courts would be for more cases to be heard on their simple merits. In these circumstances, there would be less need for lawyers to be instructed. The costs and the complexity of the law could both be reduced.

There would of course still be subjectivity in the system; it would just be the subjectivity of different people – workers, trade unionists,[6] human resource managers and employers – rather than Judges. Removing the Judge and opening up the cases to a different group of decision makers, having more in common with the Tribunal's original remit as an industrial jury, would result in different decisions being made.

It is possible to anticipate some of the likely criticisms of such a reform. Critics might say that with the loss of the specialist Judges, worse decisions would be reached, and there might be more appeals. At present, as we have seen, roughly 5 per cent of all Tribunal cases are appealed. Now this proportion might easily rise to 7 or even 10 per cent under a different system, but not to 50 per cent or 70 per cent. The reasons why more cases are not appealed is that in many cases the decision is obvious (for example, where an employer without good reason refuses to pay a former employee, or where a party has a case which looks poor on paper and fails to attend), while in other cases the parties have prepared entirely for the first-stage hearing at the Tribunal and neither side has any appetite for any further hearing. These dynamics would continue to keep the number of appeals low.

If it was said that the above system would give too much power to lay people and is therefore unworkable, it can be remarked that something like the proposed system already operates in France, where *Conseils de prud'hommes* have decided individual employment disputes for two centuries on the basis of panels containing four judges, two each from both sides of industry,[7] and in the UK in criminal and family law, where the majority of decisions are made by lay magistrates.

REFORM 3: TRIBUNAL AWARDS

Other conceivable reforms would also have an additional impact on the Tribunal system, removing some of the obstacles which have been described in previous chapters. For example, while there are genuine legal difficulties in increasing the levels of compensation for claims of unlawful discrimination (as these are common law remedies and not statutory in origin), these problems do not apply when considering the levels of compensation for cases where compensation is ordered following a finding of unfair dismissal.[8] A whole apparatus of statutory rules currently limit claimants' compensation. When calculating a claimant's entitlement under the 'basic award', the claimant's salary is capped to an arbitrary statutory limit. Given that the average salary is currently 25 per cent more than this amount, there is no good reason why this limit should not be removed. Meanwhile, the 'compensatory award' is also capped, and again there is no reason of principle (beyond a simple desire of legislators to limit employers' financial liabilities) behind this limit.

In a previous chapter, the point was also made that one reason why Tribunal awards are relatively low is that Tribunals have the power to reduce a worker's award for several different reasons, and commonly choose to employ more than one of the following reductions in any one case:

- The Tribunal can reduce the remedy paid to a worker where the worker has contributed to their own dismissal; *and*
- The Tribunal can reduce the remedy paid because it would be just and equitable to do so; *and*

- The Tribunal can reduce the remedy where a worker has failed to remedy their loss (for example, by not taking sufficient steps after dismissal to find a new job).

If the second of these powers was removed altogether, and only the first and the third retained, possibly as alternatives; the situation would be addressed where the large majority of claimants who have been successful with a claim of unfair dismissal receive awards which are significantly less than they would have been paid had they never been dismissed. The operating principle should surely be to compensate a successful worker – in all but the most exceptional cases – for their actual loss.

DEJURIDIFICATION FROM BELOW

Yet while the above reforms are desirable, the kernel of common law logic within the system must also be borne in mind. While it would be possible for Parliament to pass a law making reinstatement a more common remedy for unfair dismissal, Tribunals have the power to reinstate already. Indeed section 112 of the Employment Rights Act appears, on the face of it, to make the choice between remedy and reinstatement a decision primarily of the claimant rather than even the Tribunal:

> (1) This section applies where, on a complaint under section 111, an employment tribunal finds that the grounds of the complaint are well-founded.
> (2) The tribunal shall—
> (a) explain to the complainant what orders may be made under section 113 [i.e. orders of reinstatement and re-engagement] and in what circumstances they may be made, and
> (b) ask him whether he wishes the tribunal to make such an order.
> (3) If the complainant expresses such a wish, the tribunal may make an order under section 113.
> (4) If no order is made under section 113, the tribunal shall make an award of compensation for unfair dismissal (calculated in accordance with sections 118 to 126 to be paid by the employer to the employee …).

Yet day-to-day experience suggests that Judges fail to apply subsection (2): they do not explain to the claimant the option of reinstatement, but go briskly and directly to an assessment of financial remedies. The assumption of the Judges that reinstatement does not apply is Judge-made, not black-letter, law.

The origin of the Tribunal's hostility to reinstatement can be traced back to Kahn-Freund's intervention at the Donovan Commission, but the continuing force of the assumption against reinstatement lies also in the fact that the courts are common law courts, respecting the property rights of the employer. Were the courts really to insist on the reinstatement of a claimant, even where the respondent was set against, they would face the embarrassment of having to require an employer to take back into employment a worker that the employer was unwilling to retain.

The common sentiment of judges is that this would be an unjustifiable infringement of the employer's right to manage. If the employer is determinedly against reinstatement, the court should not order it. There must be some limit to the power of the courts, and the courts choose to set it here. In the words of one Employment Appeal Tribunal judgment (overturning a Tribunal which had ordered the reinstatement of twelve dockers dismissed for trade union activities):

> An employer in making his explanation [of why he chooses not to reinstate any particular employee] is entitled to say what in his commercial judgment is in the best interests of his business when viewed against its existence, survival and success in a competitive commercial market. That success is to be seen not only against the interests of its owners whether or not shareholders, but against the interests of the maintenance of employment and the wellbeing and contentment of its workforce ... The whole approach must be balanced between the interests of both sides of the equation. Provided that the decision or judgment of the employer is within the reasonable brackets to which we have referred it should be respected.[9]

For all the references to 'both sides' of the equation, it is clear that, for this EAT judge anyway, the dangers of inappropriate reinstatement were keener and more pressing than the dangers of requiring a worker to rot for months or years on the dole. Only in a truly exceptional case will a Tribunal impose reinstatement on an employer; the origins of the hostility to reinstatement lie deep in the common law.

Other possible reforms – for example, an increase in compensation rates for discrimination claim – are stymied by the comparison with the common law limits on compensation in parallel jurisdictions of the civil law. The reason why (for example) awards for injuries to feelings in workplace discrimination claims are to all intents and purposes capped at £30,000,[10] is that the judges in personal injury cases limit the compensation for a psychiatric injury brought on by an accident (for example, a car accident or an injury in a hospital) to around £30,000. Judges as a group would not easily consent to a system where the same accident was compensated more generously simply because the person responsible for the accident was the employer rather than a stranger. So unless the personal injury rules were reformed at the same time, no statutory reform of Tribunal compensation would be secure.

Equally, the reason that Employment Judges over-use their existing powers to reduce compensatory awards for unfair dismissal is that they have underlying common-sense notions of what the 'right' amount of award might be in any given case, which are tied to deep lying anxieties that a Tribunal system which was more generous to claimants would upset the proper relationship between workers and employers in the workplace. In the absence of much more profound social change, even any reformed scheme would founder against this obstacle.

The key weakness of the present Tribunal system is that rather than operating as an informal locus of practical decision making, it replicates the legal apparatus of the High Court or the Crown Court, albeit on a more modest scale. I have described in previous chapters instances of reforms comprehensively weakened as a result of over-exposure to the common law, including the statutory reversal of the burden of proof in discrimination cases, which has been considerably narrowed by judges.[11]

The central difficulty faced by Tribunal claimants is employment law. Of these two terms, it is not 'employment' that causes the problems, but 'law'.

RELEGATING THE LAW

In 1971, the journalist Tony Palmer was in a magistrate's court for the trial of Richard Neville, one of the editors of *Oz* magazine, and a prominent figure in the hippie counterculture of the time. Neville was accused of possessing marijuana. His trial was delayed, and Palmer turned his eye to the more mundane cases that preceded it:

> Those up in court before Neville included an Irish alcoholic, clearly unwell, clearly inarticulate, clearly desperately in need of help ... 'Speak up, I can't hear what you're saying', shouted the magistrate. It seemed to me that he harangued the defendant loudly when it suited him and then mumbled inaudibly when it suited him.

Next up was a Scotsman suffering from virulent tuberculosis. He was accused of having stolen or lost four letters belonging to his landlady: 'The man, who had difficulty in breathing properly, began to offer his explanation only to be shouted down by the magistrate and manhandled out of the dock by a police sergeant.' He had been in the wrong place; Palmer continued, he had been the wrong *class*: 'The priceless jewel of articulation, the way with words, which most of us take for granted had not been his to command. The magistrate must have known this, and so had used his own verbal, linguistic and educational advantage mercilessly.'[12]

The problems claimants face at the Tribunal are partly the same as those as these criminal defendants and also in some ways different. One connection is the difficulty of speaking in an articulate and convincing manner before any kind of court.

Now this is one of those areas where there are no absolute rules. Go before the Tribunal any day of the week and you will find claimants who can barely mutter a few words. You will also find claimants who are so loquacious that they actually weaken their case. There are even cases from time to time where a claimant refuses to address the Tribunal at all. For example, Mr D'Silva, whose case against a union was discussed in some detail in a previous chapter, opened another Tribunal case against an employer by explaining that he had sought a stay in proceedings, and since this had not been granted, he could not have a fair hearing. He then walked out. In the words of the EAT, 'It appears, however, that the [employer] was keen to obtain a decision on the substantive merits and the case accordingly proceeded, in the Appellant's absence, for no fewer than fourteen days of evidence and submissions, followed by further four days deliberation in Chambers.'[13]

But any employer (represented or unrepresented) will in general find it easier to present their case well to the Tribunal than an employee. In previous chapters, I have given different reasons for why this rule applies. The employer is likely to have a more complete knowledge of the company's decisions which led to the claim. Employers spend more on representation (not just on advocacy, but also on representation leading up to the hearing: they tend to have as a result a greater number of supportive witnesses, and their witnesses statements tend to be more detailed). Employers are usually better briefed, they have a clearer idea of what to expect from the hearing. In any large company, any given Human Resources director or any one senior manager will be more likely to have been in the Tribunal before.

In addition, employers look and sound more like Employment Judges. They fit better a Judge's notions of how a witness should appear and sound. Their class, their accent, their dress, all comply with subtle preconceptions of what constitutes reasonable and unreasonable behaviour. And it is of the nature of the common law that it gives very great freedom, indeed too much freedom, to judges to make decisions on the basis of subjective judgments as to what is reasonable or not.

The Tribunals are unlike the Magistrates' Courts of 40 years ago. They are not peopled by the sorts of defendants – or the same sort of Judges[14] – that Tony Palmer witnessed. But there is at times a hint of the same treatment, a feeling that claimants' cases will be allowed only up to a certain point, and not beyond.

WORKPLACE BARGAINING

One of the proposed reforms with which this chapter opened, was to remove the Employment Judge in favour of a system of four panellists, taking decision on a consensus basis. The more profound solution would be a similar process to that identified by the historian Willibald Steinmetz in his study of the decline of the Edwardian labour courts. Finding that the law delivered unpredictable justice, workers chose to express their complaints through collective protests instead. Ultimately, workers will have to find a way to back individual employment disputes, and make them a subject of collective bargaining rather than legal remedy.

The deepest workplace rights in the UK have invariably been won by collective struggle rather than Parliamentary debate or legal argument. The right to be paid, the right to take holidays, the right to leave an employment contract, all of these had to be won by decades or longer of struggle. As late as the 1880s and 1890s, the majority of workers in the UK worked a five-and-a-half-day week; the first football matches were accordingly scheduled for Saturday afternoons, the start of the Victorian weekend. The right to two full days away from work (as well as the accompanying right to a standard working day of eight rather than ten or more hours) was a recurring subject of labour disputes from the 1880s to 1945 and beyond.

Even in the present day, there are modest but important examples of workers winning significant improvements in their pay or conditions by a willingness to assert their rights. Forty years ago, London bus drivers were known as 'radical aristocrats' and their pay was in advance of their nearest industrial competitors: train drivers on the London Underground.[15] Today, not just tube drivers but even tube maintenance workers are paid almost double their counterparts on the buses.[16] Turnover is less among Underground workers; the employers' authority to dismiss is significantly less than on the buses. The different trajectories of the two trades can be explained, almost entirely, by the greater willingness of Underground workers to strike.

Another modest hint as to what the de-juridification of employment disputes might look like is provided by the example of a university in northern England, which saw repeated complaints of harassment by black and ethnic minority staff between 2001 and 2007. Following changes to the senior management team, and with its managers subject to intensive lobbying by the lecturers' union UCU, and by black employees, the employer agreed to survey its workers to establish whether complaints of bullying were widespread. A study showed that roughly half of the institution's black employees complained of bullying, harassment, or discrimination. In 2010, the institution adopted a rigorous 30-point action plan, intended to transform its relationship to its own workers, particularly its black workers. The vice chancellor took personal responsibility to manage the change. Training was introduced, as well as mentoring, and equality plans, not just in the institution as whole, but in each of its schools. Changes were made to the curriculum. A certain amount of managerial initiative was consciously handed back to the workers in the institution, to the black workers' group, and to the lecturers' trade union. All this was achieved by formal and informal workplace negotiation. In its outlines, this story is by no means untypical. Every day, in every region of Britain, there are employers of every size who concede tangible reforms, as a result of pressure from their workers.

Real reform must mean taking decisions out of the hands of judges and putting them back into the context of workplace bargaining. Indeed, collective bargaining needs to be used, as in the example just given, to shift power down within the workplace. If this is to be achieved, then one key agent will have to be the millions of workers who are already members of unions. None of this will happen unless ordinary workers in their millions are willing to show a greater willingness to take risks, a greater fight for equality, and a desire to return to collective protest as opposed to the over-legalisation of individual employment disputes.

Notes

PREFACE

1. I am grateful to the friends and colleagues with whom I have discussed the ideas in this book, including Richard Ascough, Sukhmani Bawa, Simon Behrman, Linda Clarke, Liz Davies, Rheian Davies, Keith Flett, Anna Macey, Steve Marsh, James Medhurst, Chris Nicholas, Dave Smith, Sarah Veale and Alexis Wearmouth. To Anne, and Sam and Ben, I owe my special thanks.
2. Employment Tribunal Field Support Office, 1st Floor, 100 Southgate Street, Bury St Edmunds, IP 33 2AQ.
3. Employment Tribunals Extension of Jurisdiction Order 1994.
4. Before 1 October 2009, the duties of the Supreme Court were vested in the judicial committee of the House of Lords, usually referred to simply as the 'House of Lords'.
5. J. Achur, *Trade Union Membership 2009* (London: Department of Business, Innovation and Skills, 2010), p. 2.
6. Ibid., p. 4.
7. *Higgins* v *Cables Montague Contracts Ltd*, EAT case 564/93.
8. Achur, *Trade Union Membership*, p. 4.
9. Ibid., p. 7.
10. Schedule A1 Trade Union and Labour Relations (Consolidation) Act 1992.
11. *NATFHE and Alliance Française de Londres*, TUR1/443/05, CAC.
12. *TGWU and Cannon Rubber Limited,* TUR1/245/03, CAC.
13. *TGWU and Convatec Ltd*, TUR1/346/04, CAC.
14. 'The common law confers no right to strike in this country. Workers who take strike action will usually be acting in breach of their contracts of employment': *National Union of Rail, Maritime & Transport Workers* v *Serco Ltd (t/a Serco Docklands)* [2011] EWCA Civ 226.
15. Sections 226–35 Trade Union and Labour Relations (Consolidation) Act 1992.
16. Section 188A Trade Union and Labour Relations (Consolidation) Act 1992.
17. Regulation 8 Fixed-Term Employees (Prevention of Less Favourable Treatment) Regulations 2002.
18. Regulation 4 Health and Safety (Consultation with Employees) Regulations 1996; or, where there is a recognised trade union, the health and safety representatives' rights are contained in regulations 3–7 of the Safety Representatives and Safety Committees Regulations 1977.
19. Schedule 1, Maternity and Parental Leave etc. Regulations 1999.
20. Occupational and Personal Pension Schemes (Consultation by Employers and Miscellaneous Amendment) Regulations 2006.
21. Regulation 13, Transfer of Undertakings (Protection of Employment) Regulations 2006.
22. Regulation 23, Working Time Regulations 1998.
23. Sections 10–15 Employment Relations Act 1999.
24. A. Pollert and A. Charlwood, 'The vulnerable worker in Britain and problems at work', *Work, Employment and Society* 23 (2009), pp. 343–62.

CHAPTER 1: THE TRIBUNAL OBSTACLE RACE

1. Respondent practitioner, cited in K.G. Knight and P.L. Latreille, 'Gender effects in British Industrial Tribunal hearings', *Industrial Law Journal* 34/4 (2005), p. 818.
2. Overheard in *Chidodo* v *DHL Services Ltd*, EAT case 0468/10.
3. 'Mum awarded £50k payout from Ironopolis Films', *Teesside Gazette*, 20 June 2008.
4. 'Sacked school assistant wins nearly £40,000 after council defies judges', *Aberdeen Press and Journal*, 12 October 2010.
5. *Daily Mail*, 11 September 2009.
6. *Employment Tribunals and EAT Statistics, 2010–2011* (London: HM Courts & Tribunals Service, 2011), p. 8; House of Commons, *Research Paper 03/87: Employment Tribunals* (London: House of Commons, 2003), p. 30.
7. Department of Trade and Industry, *Better Dispute Resolution: A Review of Employment Dispute Resolution in Great Britain* (London: DTI, 2007), p. 22.
8. S.C. Charles and P. Frisch, *Adverse Events, Stress and Litigation: A Physicians' Guide* (New York: Oxford University Press, 2005).
9. J. Aston et al., *The Experience of Claimants in Race Discrimination Employment Tribunal Cases* (London: Department of Trade and Industry, 2006), pp. 106–9. Also A. Denvir et al., *The Experiences of Sexual Orientation and Religion or Belief Discrimination Employment Tribunal Claimants* (London: Acas, 2007), p. 150.
10. Legal Aid, Sentencing and Punishment of Offenders Bill, first reading 21 July 2011.
11. Community Legal Service, *Keycard 47 – Issued April 2011* (London: Legal Services Commission, 2011), p. 1.
12. A. Griffith, 'Dramatic drop in civil legal aid eligibility', *Legal Action*, September 2008, pp. 10–11.
13. Legal Services Commission, *2010 Standard Civil Contract – Specification: Payment Annex 2010* (London: Legal Services Commission, 2010), p. 2.
14. But 'an adversarial system does not function as well as it should do, either at trial or on appeal, if the parties are not professionally represented. The risk of injustice is increased by the unrepresented litigant's failure to appreciate the need for relevant evidence and the inability of most litigants in person, through no fault of their own, to present structured legal arguments': *Launahurst Ltd* v *Arner* [2010] EWCA Civ 334.
15. It is possible to apply for legal aid for appeals.
16. M. Wynn and G. Pitt, 'The Revised Code of Practice 2010 on Time Off for Trade Union Duties and Activities: Another Missed Opportunity', *Industrial Law Journal* 39/2 (2010), pp. 209–17.
17. The Master of the Rolls publishes guideline hourly rates for solicitors and barristers. In 2011, solicitors' recommended fees varied between £111 and £409 <http://www.judiciary.gov.uk/publications-and-reports/guidance/guideline-hourly-rates/guideline-hourly-rates-2011>.
18. The form is at <http://www.employmenttribunals.gov.uk/Documents/FormsGuidance/newforms/ET1.pdf>, accessed 29 May 2011.
19. *Employment Tribunals and EAT Statistics, 2010–2011*, p. 8.
20. *Secretary of State for Trade and Industry* v *Bottrill* [1999] ICR 592, at 604.
21. Section 3A, Employment Tribunals Act 1996.

22. L. Dickens et al., *Dismissed, A Study of Unfair Dismissal and the Industrial Tribunal System* (Oxford: Basil Blackwell, 1985), p. 67.
23. *Sinclair* v *Wandsworth Council*, EAT case 0145/07.
24. *Driving Edge Limited* v *Gietowski*, EAT case 0444/07.
25. The same result occurred in *EAGA Plc* v *Tideswell* [2011], EAT case 0007/11, where the lay members outvoted the Employment Judge but were found on appeal not to have properly applied the range of reasonable responses test. Although in *Hira Company Ltd* v *Daly* [2011] EAT 0135/10, the EAT held that the panel had correctly applied the law of constructive dismissal, in finding that the employer's intention was irrelevant, in contrast to the learned Employment Judge, whose insistence on intention had been heterodox.
26. *Report of the Royal Commission on Trade Unions and Employers Associations 1965–1968* (Chairman Lord Donovan, Cmnd 3623), para 572.
27. R.M. Greenhalgh, *Industrial Tribunals, a Practical Guide* (London: IPM, 1973), p. 18.
28. *Bloxham* v *Freshfields Bruckhaus Deringer*, ET case 2205086/2006.
29. In most ETs, the witness is required when giving their evidence to sit at a separate table, typically between the parties and the panel, and sometimes to one side.
30. J. Gregory, *Trial by Ordeal: A Study of People who Lost Equal Pay and Sex Discrimination Cases in the Industrial Tribunals during 1985 and 1986* (London: Equal Opportunities Commission, 1989), pp. 25–6
31. For 'prisoner', read employer.
32. Aston et al., *The Experience of Claimants*, p. 49.
33. [1983] ICR 17, EAT.
34. *British Leyland* v *Swift* [1981] IRLR 91.
35. S.D. Anderson, *Labour Law: Management Decisions and Workers' Rights* (London: Butterworths, 2000 edn), pp. 158–70. A good illustration of the flaws of the range of reasonable responses test is provided by the case of *Reilly* v *Tayside Public Transport Company Ltd & Anor* [2011] EAT 0065/10, where the Tribunal struck out an unfair dismissal claim on the basis that the Claimant would have to overcome the range-of-reasonable-responses test, and that there was no prospect of the Claimant doing so. The EAT allowed an appeal, essentially on the basis that while the test advantages all employers it still intended to allow *some* claimants to succeed.
36. Some 47 per cent of claimants at effective full merits hearings succeeded with unfair dismissal claims in 2010–11 (*Employment Tribunals and EAT Statistics, 2010–2011*, p. 8).
37. In 2010–11, some 57 per cent of Claimants succeeded at effective full merits hearings, see *Employment Tribunals and EAT Statistics, 2010–2011*, p. 8.
38. J. Aston et al., *The Experience of Claimants in Race Discrimination Employment Tribunal Cases* (London: Department of Trade and Industry, 2006), pp. 37–9.
39. The Tribunal has for several years had the power to make recommendations; see, for example, section 65(1)(c) of the Sex Discrimination Act 1975, now codified in section 124(3) of the Equality Act 2010.
40. *Employment Tribunals and EAT Statistics, 2010–2011*, p. 9.
41. L. Dickens et al., *Dismissed: A Study of Unfair Dismissal and the Industrial Tribunal System* (Oxford: Basil Blackwell, 1985), p. 109.
42. For an example of a worker who succeeded in internal appeal, see *London Borough Of Waltham Forest* v *Martin* [2011] EAT 0069/11: where a Claimant

was dismissed by his employer after he failed a CRB-check, occasioned by his employer's own prosecution of him, which was subsequently discontinued.

43. *Employment Tribunals and EAT Statistics, 2010–2011*, p. 10.
44. Department of Trade and Industry, *Better Dispute Resolution: A Review of Employment Dispute Resolution in Great Britain* (London: DTI, 2007), p. 22.
45. The reality is not quite as harsh the figures would make it seem. Many claimants are represented by their union, or are on legal aid or a no win no fee agreement, and will pay nothing towards their costs.
46. J. McIlroy, *Industrial Tribunals: How to Take a Case, How to Win it* (London: Pluto, 1983), p. 23.
47. From 1 February 2011; the Employment Rights (Increase of Limits) Order 2010, SI 2010/2926.
48. *W. Devis & Sons Ltd* v *Atkins* [1977] IRLR 314.
49. *Polkey* v *AE Dayton Services Ltd* [1987] ICR 142. *Polkey* was a liberal judgment, before *Polkey* the Tribunal would make a finding that the dismissal was fair and the Claimant would be entitled to no remedy.
50. *Ms J Chidodo* v *DHL Services Ltd*, EAT case 0468/10.
51. *Employment Tribunals and EAT Statistics, 2010–2011*, p. 8.
52. *Sinclair Roche & Temperley (A Firm)* v *Heard & Anor* (2005), EAT case 0637/05.
53. CAB, *Empty Justice*, pp. 5–6.
54. L. Adams et al., *Research into Enforcement of Employment Tribunal Awards in England and Wales* (London: Ministry of Justice, 2009), p. 1.
55. The Register of Judgments, Orders and Fines (Amendment) Regulations 2009. Awards can be searched on the sinisterly titled website <trustonline.org.uk>.
56. Dickens et al., *Dismissed*, pp. 79, 84.

CHAPTER 2: HOW THE TRIBUNAL SYSTEM WAS ESTABLISHED

1. A. Horne, *The Mirrour of Justices* (c. 1290) (Washington, DC: John Byrne & Co., 1903 edn), p. 79.
2. H. Mantel, *Wolf Hall* (London: Fourth Estate, 2010), p. 187.
3. K.W. Wedderburn, *The Worker and the Law* (Harmondsworth: Penguin, 1965), pp. 73–88.
4. As Otto Kahn-Freund remarked, 'In Britain labour legislation is a gloss to collective bargaining', Kahn-Freund, *Labour Law: Old Traditions and New Developments* (Toronto: Clarke, Irwin & Co. Ltd., 1968), p. 32.
5. Wedderburn, *The Worker*, p. 76.
6. H.A. Turner, G. Clack and G. Roberts, *Labour Relations in the Motor Industry* (London: Allen & Unwin: 1967), p. 27.
7. K.W. Wedderburn and P.L. Davies, *Employment Grievances and Disputes Procedures in Britain* (Berkeley: University of California Press, 1969), pp. 132, 135.
8. D.R. Harris, 'Employment', in *Chitty on Contracts: The Law of Contracts. Volume II: Specific Contracts* (London: Sweet & Maxwell, 1968), pp. 631–760, here 655–6.
9. Wedderburn, *The Worker*, p. 94.
10. ILO, R119 Termination of Employment Recommendation, 1963.
11. Wedderburn, *The Worker*, p. 97.

12. Commission Secretary, 'Law and practice in other countries', 27 April 1965, LAB 28/18. All references to LAB 28 are to the papers of the Donovan Commission, which are held at the National Archives in Kew.
13. D.F. Schloss, 'State promotion of industrial peace', *Economic Journal* 3/10 (1893), pp. 218–25, 220.
14. 'Many lawyers are hardly aware of the provisions of this statute, much of which can without exaggeration be described as a very dead letter. In any event, no-one can claim that the statute has made any serious contribution to the shaping of industrial relations in this country': O. Kahn-Freund, 'A note on labour courts', para 15, June 1966, LAB 28/21.
15. *National Federation of Discharged and Demobilised Sailors and Soldiers' Bulletin*, January 1919, p. 3.
16. F. Field, 'Learning for Work, Vocational Education and Training', in R. Fieldhouse (ed.), *A History of Modern British Adult Education* (London: NIACE, 1996), pp. 333–54, here 340–44.
17. D. Robertson, *An Employer's Action Guide to Handling Industrial Tribunal Cases* (London: Kogan Page, 1977), p. 7.
18. *Angus Rhodes & Company Ltd* v *The Wool Industry Training Board* (1966) ITR 1, at 2. The Tribunal does continue to hear some Training Board cases, although they are rare, for example *On Line Design & Engineering Ltd* v *Engineering Construction Industry Training Board*, QBD (Admin), 22 October 2010.
19. In the 1965 legislation, the burden was on the employer to show that the reason for dismissal was *not* redundancy: Section 9(2)(b) Redundancy Payments Act 1965.
20. The fund continued until 1990. There is still a National Insurance Fund, from which payments can be made where an employer is insolvent; section 184 Employment Rights Act 1996.
21. Section 4A Contracts of Employment Act 1963.
22. (1966) 1 ITR 76, at 68.
23. For example, *James* v *London Borough of Greenwich* [2008] ICR 545, discussed in the next chapter.
24. Greenhalgh, *Industrial Tribunals*, p. 10.
25. Dickens et al., *Dismissed*, p. 4.
26. B. Wedderburn, 'Labour Law 2008: 40 Years On', *Industrial Law Journal* 2007 36(4), pp. 397–424, at 402–3.
27. Chairman, 'Analysis of Terms of Reference', para. 1, LAB 28/18, April 1965.
28. Ibid., para 3.
29. O. Kahn-Freund, 'Protection against arbitrary dismissal', para. 7, 19 May 1967, LAB 28/26.
30. Kahn-Freund, 'Protection against arbitrary dismissal', para. 9.
31. Ibid., appendix.
32. Minutes of meeting of 10 October 1967, para. 1, LAB 28/596.
33. Ibid., paras 8–15, LAB 28/596.
34. Minutes of meeting of 17 October 1967, paras 7–23, LAB 28/597.
35. E. Wigham, 'Division of functions of Courts, Commissions, Tribunals, etc.', October 1967, LAB 28/27; Chairman, 'Unfair dismissals, "Hybrid" cases and the limit on compensation', 18 October 1967, LAB 28/27.
36. *Report of the Royal Commission on Trade Unions and Employers Associations 1965-1968* (Chairman Lord Donovan, Cmnd 3623), paras 539–43.

37. Kahn-Freund, 'Dismissal practices in other countries', para. 16.
38. Minutes of meeting of 17 October 1967, paras 7, 13 and 23, LAB 28/597.
39. *Report of the Royal Commission on Trade Unions and Employers Associations,* paras 412–13, 415.
40. *A Fair Deal at Work* (London: Conservative Central Office, 1968), p. 63.
41. *In Place of Strife* (White Paper, 1968, Cmnd 3888), p. 36.
42. R. Darlington and D. Lyddon, *Glorious Summer: Class Struggle in Britain, 1972* (London: Bookmarks, 2001), pp. 15–24, 17.
43. Now the Certification Officer <http://www.certoffice.org>, accessed 29 May 2011.
44. Dickens et al., *Dismissed*, p. 9.
45. K. Coates and T. Topham, *The Law versus the Unions* (Nottingham: Institute for Workers' Control, 1968), p. 5.
46. *Taff Vale Railway Co* v *Amalgamated Society of Railway Servants* [1901] AC 426.
47. D. Renton, 'Class Consciousness and the Origins of Labour', *International Socialism Journal* 88 (2000), pp. 143–8; E. Hobsbawm, *Labour's Turning Point* (London: Lawrence and Wishart, 1948).
48. *Rookes v Barnard (No. 1)* [1964] AC 1129.
49. Cited in Dickens, et al., *Dismissed*, p. 217.
50. Darlington and Lyddon, *Glorious Summer*, pp. 141–77.
51. S.D. Anderman, 'Legal restrictions on Trade Unions', in S.B. Burnham and B.E. Harrell-Bond, *The Imposition of the Law* (London: Academic Press, 1979), p. 243; K.W. Wedderburn, 'Industrial Relations and the Courts', *Industrial Law Journal* 9 (1980), pp. 65–94, 83.
52. Greenhalgh, *Industrial Tribunals*, p. 22.
53. Dickens et al., *Dismissed*, p. 6.
54. *Employment Tribunals and EAT Statistics, 2010–2011* (London: HM Courts & Tribunals Service, 2011), p. 8.
55. Ibid.
56. P. Elias, 'Foreword', in J. Swift et al., *Employment Court Practice* (London: Sweet & Maxwell), 2007, p. v.
57. *Employment Tribunals and EAT Statistics, 2010–2011*, p. 8.

CHAPTER 3: AGENCY WORKERS

1. *Hersi* v *24Se7en Support Services Ltd and OCS Group UK Ltd*, ET case 2704242/2009.
2. O. Boycott and D. Hencke, 'Fear for deal on agency workers' payoffs', *Guardian*, 21 February 2009.
3. 'Agency work helps maintaining employment, facilitates job creation and enhances mobility in the labour market', European Confederation of Private Employment Agencies, Position paper, 5 May 2009.
4. D. Renton, 'Agency workers: second class?', *Socialist Lawyer*, April 2008. On 29 May 2011, the website <http://www.reed.co.uk/> was advertising a still impressive 113,000 vacancies.
5. *Government Response to Protecting Vulnerable Agency Workers Consultation* (London: BERR, 2007), p. 29.
6. H. Siddique, 'Agency workers', *Guardian,* 22 February 2008.
7. *Consistent Group Ltd* v *Kalwak & Ors* [2007] IRLR 560.

8. *Cable & Wireless Plc* v *Muscat* [2006] IRLR 354.
9. *National Grid Electricity Transmission Plc* v *Wood* (2007), EAT case 0432/07.
10. The Fixed-term Employees (Prevention of Less Favourable Treatment) Regulations 2002; The Part-time Workers (Prevention of Less Favourable Treatment) Regulations 2000.
11. I.J. Griffiths, 'The Warwick agreement', *Guardian*, 13 September 2005.
12. W.R. Cornish and G. de N. Clark, *Law and Society in England 1750–1950* (London: Sweet & Maxwell, 1989), pp. 286–9.
13. So, for example, Regulation 4 of the Working Time Regulations 1998 protects workers, not just employees, from being required to work more than 48 hours per week.
14. Section 230(1) Employment Rights Act 1996.
15. *Lane* v *Shire Roofing Co. (Oxford) Ltd.* [1995] IRLR 493.
16. Section 13(1) of the Employment Rights Act 1996 reads: 'An employer shall not make a deduction from wages of a worker … .'
17. Section 104 of the Employment Rights Act 1996 prohibits the dismissal of an employee (but not a worker) for asserting a statutory right.
18. Regulation 14, the Conduct of Employment Agencies and Employment Businesses Regulations 2003.
19. *Breakell* v *Shropshire Army Cadet Force* (2010), EAT case 0372/10; *X* v *Mid-Sussex CAB* [2011] IRLR 335.
20. *Allen (née Aboyade-Cole)* v *Hounga and another* (2011), EAT case 0329/10.
21. *Clark* v *Clark Construction Initiatives Ltd* [2008] IRLR 364.
22. The legal doctrine of privity of contract dictates that only a party to an agreement may sue on it. The theory is that agreements are reached between two parties each of which has clear entitlements and obligations. The right to sue arises from the undertaking of obligations. This model is made more difficult where agreements are between three parties as it may not be clear which party has the benefit of which of the other parties' obligations.
23. *Dacas* v *Brook Street Bureau (UK) Ltd* [2003] IRLR 358, paragraph 13.
24. Ibid., paragraph 75.
25. [1989] 1 Lloyd's Rep 213.
26. *Cable & Wireless Plc* v *Muscat* [2006], paragraph 43.
27. More recently a Lord Justice sitting in the Court of Appeal.
28. *James v London Borough of Greenwich* [2007] IRLR 168, EAT.
29. Ibid., paragraph 59.
30. Ibid., paragraph 56.
31. Ibid., paragraph 57.
32. See Chapter 8, below.
33. *James* v *London Borough of Greenwich* [2008] ICR 545, CA, paragraph 55.
34. Agency workers were found not to be employees in *Action Contracts (East Midlands) Ltd* v *Ablitt & Anor*, EAT case 0568/07; *Astbury* v *Bentley Motors*, EAT case 1844/06; *Beck* v *London Borough of Camden*, EAT case 0121/08; *Craigie* v *London Borough of Haringey*, EAT case 0556/06; *East Living Ltd* v *Sridhar*, EAT case 0476/07; *Heatherwood and Wrexham Park NHS Hospitals NHS Trust* v *Kulubowila and Ors*, EAT case 0633/06 *Muschett* v *HM Prison Service*, EAT case 0132/08; and *Wood Group Engineering (North Sea)* v *Robertson*, EAT case 0081/06. A finding of employee status was made in *Consistent Group Ltd* v *Kalwak & Ors*, note 7, above, but was overturned

by the Court of Appeal: *Consistent Group Ltd* v *Kalwak & Ors* [2008] EWCA Civ 430.

35. *James* v *London Borough of Greenwich* [2006], paragraph 61.
36. 'EU ministers discuss agency staff rights', *Guardian*, 5 December 2007.
37. *The Protecting Vulnerable Agency Workers Consultation* (London: BERR, 2007).
38. D. Hencke, 'Minister blocks job rights bill', *Guardian*, 3 March 2007.
39. P. Wintour, 'Agency and temporary workers win rights deal', *Guardian*, 21 May 2008.
40. 'Agency Workers: Joint Declaration by Government, the CBI and the TUC', Department of Business, Enterprise and Regulatory Reform, press release, 20 May 2008.
41. Regulations 5–8, Agency Worker Regulations 2010.
42. Written Ministerial Statement, 19 October 2010.
43. Regulation 17 of the Agency Worker Regulations 2010 does protect workers against victimisation including dismissal; so where a worker is dismissed for having brought an equal treatment claim under the Regulations, that dismissal would be unfair.
44. *Employment Agencies. Implementation of the Agency Workers Directive: A Consultation Paper* (London: Department of Business, Innovation and Skill, 2009), paragraph 1.10. Emphasis added.

CHAPTER 4: EQUAL PAY

1. Sir Stuart Rose, Chief Executive, Marks & Spencer, cited in *Observer*, 31 May 2009.
2. Women & Work Commission, *Shaping a Fairer Future: Three Years On* (London: Government Equalities Office, 2009), p. 5.
3. *Annual Statistics for the Tribunals Service 2009–10* (London: Tribunals Service, 2010), p. 22; *Employment Tribunal and EAT Statistics 1 April 2007 to 31 March 2008* (London: Department for Business, Innovation and Skills, 2009), p. 2; *Employment Tribunal and EAT Statistics 1 April 2006 to 31 March 2007* (London: Department for Business, Enterprise and Regulatory Reform, 2007), p. 2.
4. R. Pike, *Patterns of Pay: Results of the Annual Survey of Hours and Earnings 1997 to 2010* (London: Office for National Statistics, 2011), p. 14.
5. *Labour Market Statistics, June 2009* (London: Office of National Statistics, 2009), p. 20.
6. Women & Work Commission, *Shaping a Fairer Future*, p. 5.
7. 'Equal pay', *UCU Equality Extra*, June 2006; 'How much are you worth?', *Times Higher Education Supplement*, 13 March 2008.
8. S. Faludi, *Backlash: The Undeclared War Against American Women* (New York: Doubleday, 1991).
9. *Archibald* v *Fife Council* [2004] IRLR 651; D. Renton, 'A new era for equality law? *Archibald v Fife Council* reconsidered', *Disability and Society*, 21/7 (2006), pp. 709–20.
10. *Mayor and Burgesses of the London Borough of Lewisham* v *Malcolm* [2008] UKHL 43; D. Renton, 'Malcolm in the middle: disability setback', *Socialist Lawyer*, September 2008.
11. *Allonby* v *Accrington and Rossendale College and Ors* [2004] IRLR 224.

12. *McAvoy and Ors* v *South Tyneside Borough Council and Ors*, EAT case 0006/08.
13. *Walton Centre for Neurology & Neurosurgery NHS Trust* v *Bewley* [2008] IRLR 588.
14. *Ministry of Defence* v *Armstrong* [2004] IRLR 672.
15. *Preston & Ors* v *Wolverhampton Healthcare NHS Trust (No. 3)* [2006] ICR 606.
16. [2007] IRLR 576.
17. *Equal Opportunities Commission* v *Secretary of State for Trade & Industry* [2007] EWHC 483 (Admin).
18. Sex Discrimination Act 1975 (Amendment) Regulations 2008.
19. Upholding the decision in *Webb* v *EMO Air Cargo (UK) Ltd* [1995] ICR 1021.
20. This wording is retained in section 26 of the Equality Act 2010.
21. Section 65(1) Equality Act 2010.
22. Equal pay claims can be bought after the expiry of six months in the civil courts: *Abdulla & Ors* v *Birmingham City Council* [2010] EWHC 3303 (QB).
23. *South Tyneside Metropolitan Borough Council* v *Anderson and Ors* [2007] IRLR 715; *Robertson and Ors* v *Department for Environment, Food and Rural Affairs* [2005] IRLR 363.
24. *Edmonds* v *Computer Services (South West) Ltd* [1977] IRLR 359.
25. *Tyldesley* v *TML Plastics Ltd* [1996] ICR 356.
26. *Christie and others* v *John E Haith Ltd* [2003] IRLR 670.
27. *Redcar and Cleveland Borough Council* v *Bainbridge and Ors (No 1)* [2007] IRLR 984.
28. *Rutherford* v *Secretary of State for Trade and Industry (No 2)* [2006] IRLR 551.
29. Tribunals Service, *Employment Tribunal and EAT Statistics (GB) 1 April 2009 to 31 March 2010* (London: Tribunals Service), pp. 5–7.
30. *Middlesbrough Council* v *Surtees and Ors*, EAT case 0417/07.
31. *Addis* v *Gramophone Co.* [1909] A.C. 488.
32. *Chief Constable of West Yorkshire* v *Vento* [2002] EWCA Civ 1871.
33. Employment Rights (Increase of Limits) Order 2010, SI 2010/2926.
34. *Annual Statistics for the Tribunals Service 2009–10*, p. 22; *Employment Tribunal and EAT Statistics 1 April 2007 to 31 March 2008*, p. 2; *Employment Tribunal and EAT statistics 1 April 2006 to 31 March 2007*, p. 2.
35. For example, K. Higginbottom, 'Pay and display', *Guardian*, 5 July 2008.
36. S. Cross, 'What good are no-win no-fee lawyers?', *Equal Opportunities Review*, March 2008, pp. 18–22, 19.
37. In one high-profile equal value case, the comparison was made between (typically female) speech therapists and (typically male) clinical psychologists (*Enderby* v *Frenchay Health Authority and Secretary of State for Health* [1993] IRLR 591), in another case (typically female) nursery nurses and (typically male) clerical workers (*Leverton* v *Clywyd County Council* [1989] IRLR 28).
38. See the discussion of attendance allowances, overtime, or unsocial hours payments in *St Helens & Knowsley Hospitals NHS Trust* v *Brownbill & Ors* [2011] EWCA Civ 903, at paragraphs 15–16.
39. In 2007, the pay gap in financial mediation, at 40.3 per cent was roughly three times the gap in health and local government: J.R. Shackleton, *Should we Mind the Gap?* (London: Institute of Economic Affairs, 2008), p. 28.
40. B. McKenna, 'The union perspective on equal pay', *Equal Opportunities Review*, March 2008, pp. 13–17, 13.

41. N. Cohen, 'A lawyer's help to underpaid women is putting the wind up trade unions', *Observer*, 18 June 2006.
42. 'Law 100: the UK's most powerful lawyers', *The Times*, 22 April 2008.
43. *Allen & Ors* v *GMB* [2008] IRLR 690.
44. 'Thousands in line for cash after equal pay ruling', *Daily Record*, 22 December 2008.
45. J. Kelly, *Rethinking Industrial Relations* (London: Routledge, 1998).
46. McKenna, 'The union perspective', p. 14.
47. *Allen & Ors* v *GMB*.
48. 'GMB lose Allen Case', *John's Labour blog* <http:// grayee.blogspot.com/2008/07/gmb-lose-allen-case.html>, 16 July 2008, accessed 29 May 2011.
49. S. Basketter, 'Single status judgment', *Socialist Worker*, 26 July 2008.
50. 'Unison NEC report to London region', *Jon's union blog* <http://jonrogers1963.blogspot.com>, 1 March 2009, accessed 29 May 2011.
51. N. Hodgson, 'Amnesty call over equal pay claims', *Liverpool Echo*, 15 October 2007.
52. L. Peacock, 'Equality commission calls for equal pay review', *Personnel Today*, 16 March 2009.
53. S. Sagall, 'When history was made in Dagenham', *Socialist Review*, October 2010.

CHAPTER 5: WHY DO SO FEW RACE CASES WIN?

1. *Employment Tribunals and EAT Statistics, 2010–2011* (London: HM Courts & Tribunals Service, 2011), p. 8.
2. *R (on the application of E)* v *Governing Body of JFS and the Admissions Appeal Panel of JFS and others* [2009] UKSC 15.
3. *Coleman* v *Attridge* Law Case C-303/06, ECJ.
4. *Zarczynska* v *Levy* [1979] ICR 184.
5. *Showboat Entertainment Centre* v *Owens* [1984] ICR 65.
6. *Redfearn* v *Serco Ltd* [2005] IRLR 744, at 748.
7. *Redfearn* v. *Serco Ltd* [2006] IRLR 623.
8. *Chattopadhyay* v *Headmaster of Holloway School* [1982] ICR 132.
9. *King* v *Great Britain-China Centre* [1992] ICR 516. In *King*, the view of the court was that the reverse burden of proof was a power available to be used at the court's discretion; in contrast to *Chattopadhyay*, where it was held that the inference applied as a matter of course.
10. Article 10, Council Directive 2000/78/EC.
11. *Re B (Minors) (Sexual Abuse: Standard of Proof)* [2008] UKHL 35.
12. For example, in criminal prosecutions for breaches of section of the Health and Safety at Work Act 1974, section 40 of the Act imposes a reverse burden.
13. *Appiah* v *Bishop Douglas Roman Catholic High School* [2007] EWCA Civ 10, emphasis in the original.
14. The reverse burden of proof applies to all discrimination claims, in like terms to race cases.
15. *Madarassy* v *Nomura International plc* [2007] IRLR 246.
16. 'Ethnic staff suffer 12% pay gap', *Times Higher Education Supplement*, 31 May 2002; '"Black pay gap" robs minorities of £7,000 a year', *Observer*, 21 November 2004.

17. In the fourth quarter of 2008, 11 per cent of black workers were unemployed, in contrast to 6 per cent of white workers. TUC, *Black Workers and the Recession* (London: Trade Union Congress, 2009), p. 7.
18. *Anya* v *University Of Oxford & Anor*, EAT case 39/98.
19. *Anya* v *University of Oxford & Anor* [2001] EWCA Civ 405.
20. *King* v *Great Britain-China Centre; Igen Ltd & Ors* v *Wong*, EAT case 0944/03; and *Qureshi* v *Victoria University Of Manchester & Anor* [2001] ICR 863.
21. *Qureshi* v *Victoria University Of Manchester & Anor* [2001] ICR 863.
22. In ordinary French civil proceedings, submissions are made in writing rather than orally.
23. Based on A. Good, *Anthropology and Expertise in the Asylum Courts* (London: Routledge, 2007), p. 198.
24. Ibid., pp. 190–98, 197.
25. In 2007, the Ministry of Justice proposed that Employment and Immigration Judges should be "cross-ticketed", in other words that the same Judges should be able to appear in either category of case: *Implementing Part 1 of the Tribunals, Courts and Enforcement Act 2007* (London: Ministry of Justice, 2007), pp. 32–3.

CHAPTER 6: HUMAN RIGHTS DECISIONS IN THE TRIBUNAL

1. J. Coppel, 'I'm an Employment Lawyer, What has the Human Rights Act done for me?', paper presented to the Human Rights Lawyers Association, 27 April 2005, p. 1.
2. C.K. Lee, *Against the Law: Labor Protests in China's Rustbelt and Sunbelt* (Berkeley: University of California Press, 2007), p. 187.
3. B. Simpson, *Human Rights and the End of Empire: Britain and the Genesis of the European Convention* (Oxford: Oxford University Press, 2001).
4. This list is based on R. Allen, R. Crasnow and A. Beale, *Employment Law and Human Rights* (Oxford: Oxford University Press, 2007), p. 20.
5. [2004] UKHL 56.
6. [2010] UKSC 45.
7. *Harrow London Borough Council* v *Qazi* [2003] UKHL 43; *Kay* v *Lambeth London Borough Council* [2006] UKHL, and *Doherty* v *Birmingham City Council* [2008] UKHL 57.
8. *McCann* v *United Kingdom* (2008) 47 EHRR 913.
9. *Kay* v *United Kingdom*, application number 3572/06.
10. *Klass* v *Germany* (1978) 2 EHRR 214.
11. *Funke* v *France* (1933) 16 EHRR 297.
12. *Campbell* v *MGN Ltd* [2004] UKHL 22.
13. Article 11(2) provides exceptions along similar lines to article 8(2).
14. *Malik* v *Waltham Forest PCT & Secretary of State for Health* [2006] EWHC 487. Article 1 has also been applied to private pensions (*X* v *Sweden* (1986) 8 EHRR 252) and to employment-related welfare benefits (*Stec and others* v *UK* (2006) 20 BHRC 348).
15. (1997) 24 EHRR 523, paragraph 45.
16. 45 EHRR 37.
17. *Copland* v *UK*, paragraph 43.
18. [2002] IRLR 568.
19. *Wilson* v *Palmer*, paragraph 46.

20. *Vasquez* v *The Queen* [1994] 1 WLR 1304, *Regina* v *Lambert* [2001] UKHL 37, at 81.
21. *Attridge Law* v *Coleman* [2010] ICR 242, EAT, at 257B–C, emphasis added.
22. [2004] IRLR 625.
23. That is, the principle in *Iceland Frozen Food* v *Jones*, discussed in Chapter 1.
24. For example, in article 1 of the Convention: 'The High Contracting Parties [that is, the signatory states] shall secure to everyone within their jurisdiction the rights and freedoms defined in Section I of this Convention.'
25. *X* v *Y*, paragraph 57.
26. Ibid., Paragraph 69.
27. Permission to appeal to the Court of Appeal was refused: [2005] EWCA Civ 295.
28. [2004] IRLR 129, paragraph 32.
29. Application No 32792/05, [2009] IRLR 139.
30. [2005] IRLR 811.
31. *Copsey* v *Devon Clays,* paragraph 39.
32. *R (on the application of G)* v *X School Governors* [2010] IRLR 222. In *Puri* v *Bradford Teaching Hospitals* [2011] EWHC 970 (Admin), it was found that article 6 is not engaged in ordinary internal disciplinary procedures where their effect will not be to deprive the employee of her right to practise her profession.
33. *Fosh* v *Cardiff University* [2009] EWCA Civ 38.
34. 'The Convention was intended primarily to protect civil and political, rather than economic and social, rights': *N* v *United Kingdom*, [2008] ECHR 453, paragraph 24.
35. Coppel, 'I'm an Employment Lawyer', p. 1.
36. As observed in *Whittaker* v *Watson* [2002] ICR 1244.

CHAPTER 7: UNIONS AND THE LAW

1. An anonymous Tribunal judge quoted in L. Dickens et al., *Dismissed: A study of unfair Dismissal and the Industrial Tribunal System* (Oxford: Basil Blackwell, 1985), p. 68.
2. J. McIlroy, *Industrial Tribunals: How to Take a Case, How to Win it* (London: Pluto, 1983), p. 1.
3. In fact, as we saw in Chapter 1, around three-fifths of Tribunal claims are won by workers.
4. 'Karen Reissmann NHS whistleblower Tribunal is settled', *Socialist Worker*, 3 February 2009; also 'Nurse's deal over "unfair sacking"', *Manchester Evening News*, 28 January 2009.
5. J.R. Shackleton, *Employment Tribunals: Their Growth and the Case for Radical Reform* (London: Institute of Economic Affairs, 2002), p. 45.
6. O. Kahn-Freund, 'Protection against arbitrary dismissal', para 7, 19 May 1967, LAB 28/26, appendix.
7. C. Kimber, 'In the balance: the class struggle in Britain', *International Socialism* 122 (2009), pp. 33–64.
8. These figures are derived from the various union annual reports for 2008, which are published on the website of the Certification Officer <http://www.certoffice.org>, accessed 1 March 2009.

9. For example, the very high costs incurred by the British Air Lines Pilot Association (BALPA) in bringing *British Airways Plc* v *Williams and Ors* [2008] ICR 779.
10. Dickens et al., *Dismissed*, p. 31.
11. The total size of the UK workforce is around 30 million workers. A 2 per cent dismissal rate is equivalent to 600,000 dismissals in a normal year. In August 2011, the Office for National Statistics recorded that redundancies were running at the rate of 154,000 a quarter; and while these were relatively high figures compared to what might be expected in a boom, this of course recorded only one category of dismissals, redundancies, and not dismissals for retirement, capability, conduct, and so on: Office for National Statistics, 'Labour market statistical bulletin', August 2011, p. 10.
12. Department of Trade and Industry, *Better Dispute Resolution: A Review of Employment Dispute Resolution in Great Britain* (London: DTI, 2007), p. 22.
13. N. Cunningham, 'What will my hearing cost?', <http://etclaims.co.uk/?s=cost+representation>, 7 December 2008, accessed 29 May 2011.
14. Email to the author, 20 April 2011.
15. In 2006, the AUT merged with the other main union in the sector, the National Association of Teachers in Further and Education (NATFHE) to form the University and Colleges Union (UCU).
16. J. Shepherd, '14,000 British professors – but only 50 are black', *Guardian*, 27 May 2011.
17. H. Singh, *I or We? Generating Futures* (London: Association of University Teachers, 2004), p. 4.
18. Ibid., p. 15.
19. Ibid., p. 20.
20. Ibid., p. 21.
21. Ibid., p. 6.
22. Sections 16 and 46–55, Trade Union and Labour Relations (Consolidation) Act 1992.
23. *British Medical Association* v *Chaudhury* [2007] EWCA Civ 788.
24. Ibid., paragraph 155.
25. *D'Silva* v *NATFHE (now known As University and College Union) & Ors* (2008), EAT 0384/07.
26. Ibid., paragraph 32.
27. <http://sites.google.com/site/cemkumar/>, accessed 29 May 2011.
28. *GMB* v *Allen*, EAT, paragraphs 18–19.
29. *Allen* v *GMB*, CA, paragraph 12.
30. *British Airways Plc* v *Unite the Union* [2010] IRLR 809. Also *National Union of Rail, Maritime & Transport Workers* v *Serco Ltd (t/a Serco Docklands)* [2011] EWCA Civ 226.
31. J. Kelly, *Rethinking Industrial Relations: Mobilization, Collectivism and Long Waves* (London: Routledge, 1998), pp. 83–105.
32. A. Alexander, 'The gravedigger of dictatorship', *Socialist Review*, March 2011.
33. J. Plunkett, *Growth Without Pain? The Faltering Living Standards of People on Low-to-Middle Incomes* (London: Resolution Foundation, 2011), p. 10.
34. CIPD, *Employee Outlook: Summer 2011* (London: CIPD, 2011), p. 12.
35. Office for National Statistics, 'Consumer price indices', 16 August 2011.

CHAPTER 8: THE COMMON LAW

1. F. Engels, 'The English Constitution', *Vorwärts*, 18 September 1844.
2. A.C.L. Davies, 'Judicial Self-Restraint in Labour Law', *Industrial Law Journal* 38/3 (2009), pp. 278–305, 287.
3. S. Anderman, 'The Interpretation of Protective Employment Statutes and Contracts of Employment', *Industrial Law Journal* 29 (2000), pp. 223–42.
4. M. Berlins and C. Dyer, *The Law Machine* (London: Penguin, 1994 edn), pp. 71–2.
5. Different rules apply where the claim is for discrimination rather than wrongful or unfair dismissal.
6. *Addis* v. *Gramophone Co.* [1909] A.C. 488, HL.
7. Lord Shaw, for example, was born in 1850.
8. W. Steinmetz, *Begegnungen vor Gericht Eine Sozial- und Kulturgeschicte des englischen Arbeitsrechts 1850–1925* (Munich: R. Oldenbourg, 2002), p. 264.
9. W.R. Cornish and G. de N. Clark, *Law and Society in England 1750–1950* (London: Sweet & Maxwell, 1989), pp. 286–9.
10. *Dunnachie* v *Kingston upon Hull City Council* [2004] ICR 1052.
11. Steinmetz, *Begegnungen*, pp. 242–3, 247.
12. Ibid., p. 280.
13. Ibid., p. 322.
14. Ibid., p. 265.
15. Ibid., p. 320.
16. Ibid., p. 641.
17. J. McIlroy, *Industrial Tribunals: How to Take a Case, How to Win it* (London: Pluto, 1983), p. 22.
18. *Caparo Industries plc* v *Dickman* [1990] 2 AC 605.
19. *Hagan and Ors* v *ICI Chemicals & Olymers Ltd* [2002] IRLR 31.
20. *British Leyland (UK) Ltd* v *Swift* [1981] IRLR 91.
21. *British Home Stores* v *Burchell* [1978] IRLR 379.
22. Section 111(2) of the Employment Rights Act 1996.
23. P.S. Atiyah, in J. Conaghan and W. Mansell, *The Wrongs of Tort* (London: Pluto, 1999), p. 52.
24. *Royal Bank of Scotland* v *Theobald*, EAT case 0444/06.
25. *Royal Bank of Scotland* v *Bevan*, EAT case 0440/07.
26. *National Union of Rail, Maritime & Transport Workers* v *Serco Ltd (t/a Serco Docklands)* [2011] EWCA Civ 226, paragraph 7.
27. J. Conaghan and W. Mansell, *The Wrongs of Tort* (London: Pluto, 1999), pp. 124–59; also Cornish and Clark, *Law and Society*, pp. 154–8.
28. *Sturges* v *Bridgman* (1879), 11 Ch.D 852 at p. 865.
29. 'Twenty-two years ago, there was not a single judge sitting in the EAT who was an employment law specialist at the bar. In 1985, the EAT was staffed by a group of courtly Oxbridge-educated male judges with scarcely the slightest understanding of discrimination law issues. In 2007, the EAT is staffed by a group of courtly Oxbridge-educated male judges with a deep understanding of discrimination law issues. Some things change, others do not': M. Rubinstein, 'My back pages', *Equal Opportunities Review*, March 2007, pp. 25–8, 28.
30. *Convergent Telecom* v *Swann and anor*, EAT case 534/02.
31. *Echendu* v *William Morrisson Supermarkets Plc*, EAT case 1675/07.
32. *Post Office* v *Sanhotra*, EAT case 1374/98.

33. *Qureshi* v *Victoria University of Manchester*, EAT case 484/95.
34. A. Gramsci, *Selections from Prison Notebooks* (London: Lawrence and Wishart, 1971), pp. 323–33.
35. A. Supiot, *Homo Juridicus: On the Anthropological Function of the Law* (London: Verso, 2007), pp. 78–110.
36. *Printing and Numerical Registering Company v Sampson* (1875) 19 Eq. 462, 464; E. Pashukanis, *Law and Marxism: A General Theory.* (London: Pluto, 1989), p. 121.
37. *Shogun Finance Limited* v *Hudson (FC)* [2003] UKHL 62.
38. *Carmichael & anor* v *National Power plc* [2000] IRLR 43.
39. *White* v *Reflecting Roadstuds Ltd* [1991] IRLR 331.
40. *Crossley* v *Faithful & Gould Holdings Ltd* [2004] ICR 1615.
41. G. Robertson, *The Tyrannicide Brief* (London: Vintage, 2006), pp. 218–24.
42. R.M. Greenhalgh, *Industrial Tribunals, A Practical Guide* (London: IPM, 1973), p. 22.
43. *James* v *London Borough of Greenwich* [2007] IRLR 168, emphasis added.

CHAPTER 9: EMPLOYMENT TRIBUNALS IN CRISIS?

1. R.M. Greenhalgh, *Industrial Tribunals, A Practical Guide* (London: IPM, 1973), p. 20.
2. K. Hopkins, 'Recession set to burden employment tribunals', *Observer*, 5 July 2009.
3. K. McGill, 'Tribunal system struggling as claims rise', *Scotsman*, 24 September 2001; M. Watts, 'Tribunal cases soar as staff use the law on the working week', *Independent*, 30 July 2006; 'Rise in sex discrimination claims', *BBC News*, 21 September 2007; 'What can be done to end rise in tribunals?', *Personnel Today*, 19 February 2002; 'Fury at soaring bills for tribunals', *Evening Chronicle* [Birmingham], 2 March 2004.
4. B. Clement, '"Compensation culture" sweeping Britain', *Independent*, 13 September 2004.
5. 'Number of businesses down', Office for National Statistics, 27 September 2010.
6. R. Gribben, 'Rise in unfair dismissal claims during recession', *Telegraph*, 23 July 2009; K. Hopkins, 'Recession set to burden employment tribunals', *Observer*, 5 July 2009.
7. A. Hirsch and S. Boseley, 'Swine flu pandemic could fuel rise in workplace litigation', *Guardian*, 27 July 2009; T. Craig, 'Swine flu pandemic raises workplace litigation risk', *Personnel Today* , 28 July 2009.
8. Tribunals Service, *Employment Tribunal and EAT Statistics (GB) 1 April 2008 to 31 March 2009* (London: Tribunals Service, 2009), p. 6.
9. 'Unfair dismissal and redundancy tribunal claims rocket', *Personnel Today*, 30 September 2009; D. Woods, 'Unfair dismissal claims rise by almost a third since 2008', *Human Resources*, 1 October 2009.
10. 'Employment law queries cost small businesses £2.4bn a year', *Travel Weekly*, 17 September 2009.
11. *Legal Aid: Refocusing on Priority Cases* (London: Ministry of Justice, 2009), p. 7.

12. S. Green, 'Protection of jobs "is at tipping point"', *The Journal* [Newcastle], 7 July 2009; B. Digby, *Jobs for the Future: The Business Vision for Sustainable Employment in the UK* (London: CBI, 2009), p. 44.
13. Digby, *Jobs for the Future*, p. 44.
14. *Explanatory Memorandum to the Sex Discrimination (Amendment of Legislation) Regulations 2008* (London: Government Equalities Office, 2008), p. 32.
15. *Employment Regulation: Up to the Job?* (London: British Chambers of Commerce, 2010), p. 9.
16. DTI, *Better Dispute Resolution*, pp. 7, 21.
17. The Employment Act 2002 (Dispute Resolution) Regulations 2004.
18. Department of Trade and Industry, *Full Regulatory Impact Assessment: Statutory Dispute Resolution Procedures* (London: DTI, 2004), p. 11.
19. P. Davies and M. Freedland, *Towards a Flexible Labour Market: Labour Legislation and Regulations since the 1990s* (Oxford: Clarendon, 2007), p. 249.
20. Employment Tribunal Service, *Annual reports and accounts 2003–4* (London: Department of Trade and Industry, 2004), p. 23; *Employment Tribunal and EAT Statistics (GB) 1 April 2007 to 31 March 2008*, p. 2.
21. 'And here the right policy is to combine the most modern and flexible competition regime including, as announced today, the further extension of risk based regulation – into Employment Tribunals – with the most effective incentives and support for British investment and British innovation': Her Majesty's Treasury, *Chancellor of the Exchequer's Budget Statement*, press release, 21 March 2007.
22. Department of Trade and Industry, *Better Dispute Resolution: A Review of Employment Dispute Resolution in Great Britain* (London: DTI, 2007), p. 4.
23. Ibid., p. 22.
24. *Employment Tribunals and EAT Statistics, 2010–2011* (London: HM Courts & Tribunals Service, 2011), p. 8; *Employment Tribunal and EAT Statistics (GB) 1 April 2007 to 31 March 2008*, p. 3; House of Commons, *Research Paper 03/87: Employment Tribunals* (London: House of Commons, 2003), p. 30; *Employment Tribunals: LRD's Guide to the New Procedures*, p. 2; Employment Tribunal Service, *Annual Report and Accounts 1999–2000* (London: ETS, 2000), p. 11.
25. L. Dickens et al., *Dismissed: A Study of Unfair Dismissal and the Industrial Tribunal System* (Oxford: Basil Blackwell, 1985), p. 31.
26. N. Meagre et al., *Awareness, Knowledge and Exercise of Individual Rights* (London: DTI, 2002),
27. Cited at DTI, *Better Dispute Resolution*, p. 15.
28. R. Dinghy, untitled paper presented to the 2007 Industrial Law Society Conference, Oxford, 14–16 September 2007.
29. T. Potbury, 'Simplifying is not always so easy to do', *Personnel Today*, 24 July 2007.
30. ACAS – Code of Practice 1 – Disciplinary and Grievance Procedures.
31. Schofield, 'Effective resolution of employment disputes'.
32. J. Guthrie, 'Deliver us from Employment Tribunal Hell', *Financial Times*, 18 July 2007; also see 'Workplace mediation turning nasty as new rules backfire', *Observer*, 22 May 2007; 'Workplace dispute rules to be repealed', *Telegraph*, 22 May 2007, and 'Brown targets Tribunals', *Sunday Times*, 18 May 2002.

33. *Fair Play on Women's Pay* (London: Conservative Party, 2007). The government belatedly announced a consultation in May 2011 of plans along these lines, *Consultation on Modern Workplaces* (London: Department of Business, Innovation and Skills, 2011).
34. 'Business', *The Conservative Manifesto 2010.*
35. Section 21, Immigration, Asylum and Nationality Act 2006.
36. H. Giles, 'Stop legal creatures feeding on small businesses', *The Times*, 3 January 2011.
37. H. Giles, 'Bosses must again have power to hire and fire', *The Times*, 13 May 2011.
38. *Employment Tribunals and EAT Statistics, 2010–2011*, p. 8.
39. Office for National Statistics, 'Number of businesses down'.
40. *Resolving Workplace Disputes: A Consultation* (London: Department of Business, Innovation and Skills, 2010); also ibid., p. 1.
41. *An Employers' Charter: For Unfair Treatment; Increased Job Insecurity and Limited Access to Justice* (London: TUC, 2011), p. 3.
42. *R* v *Secretary of State for Employment ex parte Seymour-Smith and Perez (No.2)* [2000] IRLR 263. Although the two-year period was found to be indirectly discriminatory, it was also found to be capable of justification.
43. See the table at note 30, above.
44. For the continuity between the present proposals and the Gibbons report, see *Resolving Workplace Disputes: A Consultation*, p. 3.
45. The burden on claimants to submit a claim in time is set out in the previous chapter. For the respondent's burden, see *Kwik Save Stores Ltd* v *Swain & Ors* [1997] ICR 49 and *Moroak t/a Blake Envelopes v Cromie* (2005) IRLR 535.
46. *Resolving Workplace Disputes: Impact Assessment*, p.147.
47. A. Denvir et al., *The Experience of Sexual Orientation and Religion or Belief Discrimination Employment Tribunal Claimants* (London: ACAS, 2007), pp. 98–9.
48. K. Armstrong and D. Coats, *The Costs and Benefits of Employment Tribunal Cases for Employers and Claimants* (London: Department of Trade and Industry, 2007), p. 14.
49. *Anyanwu and Another* v *South Bank Student Union and Another And Commission For Racial Equality* [2001] IRLR 305.
50. *Mehta* v *Child Support Agency*, EAT case 0127/10.
51. *Resolving Workplace Disputes: Impact Assessment*, p. 51.
52. The consultation document based this figure almost entirely on proposals 1) and 11). There was no accounting for the losses to workers in terms of reduced claims as a result of the anxiety caused by issuing fees or the greater use of costs orders.
53. Albeit while retaining protection for discrimination claims.
54. 'Legal Aid Reform: Cumulative Impact', *Proposals for the Reform of Legal Aid in England and Wales* (London: Ministry of Justice, 2010).
55. Judges' Council of England and Wales, Response of a sub-committee of the Judges' Council to the Government's Consultation Paper CP12/10, 'Proposals for the Reform of Legal Aid in England and Wales' (London: JCEW, 2001), p. 8.
56. *Gayle* v *Sandwell & West Birmingham NHS Trust* [2011] EWCA Civ 924, paragraph 20.

CONCLUSION: HOW COULD TRIBUNALS BE REFORMED?

1. Judge Bridoison in F. Rabelais, *Complete Works* (Berkeley: University of California Press, 1991), p. 379.
2. C. Dickens, *Bleak House* (London: Forgotten Books, 2008), p. 5.
3. As is the case in Germany and Italy, J.R. Shackleton, *Employment Tribunals: Their Growth and the Case for Radical Reform* (London: Institute of Economic Affairs, 2002), p. 32.
4. Or workers dismissed for whistleblowing.
5. Section 128, Employment Rights Act 1996.
6. For the employee side to be properly heard in a reconstituted Tribunal system, there should be a wider discussion of the decision taken by 'employee' panelists. It used to be that such panelists had to be recommended by a union; more recently, the Tribunal system has recruited both 'employee' and 'employer' panelists on an individual basis. Where employee panelists do come from a union background; it is striking that very few make any attempt to report to their union on the cases they have heard or the decisions they have made.
7. R. Oautrat and R. le Roux-Cocheril, *Les conseils de prud'hommes* (Paris: Éditions Sirey, 1984).
8. Even if reinstatement was to become the primary remedy for unfair dismissal, there would still need to be some rules for calculating remedies for that group of workers who did not seek reinstatement.
9. *Port of London Authority* v *Payne & Ors* (1992), EAT case 511/91. Also see *DB Schenker Rail (UK) Ltd* v *Doolan* [2010] EAT 0053/09, where a Tribunal was said to have erred in merely ordering reinstatement to a company pension scheme.
10. *Vento* v *Chief Constable of West Yorkshire Police* [2002] EWCA Civ 1871, as subject to an uplift for inflation, in *Da'Bell* v *National Society for the Prevention of Cruelty to Children* [2009] IRLR 19.
11. See the discussion in Chapter 5 above.
12. T. Palmer, *The Trials of Oz* (London: Blond and Briggs, 1971), p. 15.
13. *D'Silva* v *NATFHE (now known As University and College Union) & Ors* [2008] IRLR 412, paragraph 19.
14. J.A.G. Griffiths, *The Politics of the Judiciary* (London: Fontana, 1997).
15. K. Fuller, *Radical aristocrats: London bus workers from the 1880s to the 1980s* (London: Lawrence and Wishart, 1985).
16. The tube drivers' union Aslef gives the starting salary of a tube driver as £42,424.00 or £815 per week, see <http://www.aslef.org.uk/information/102222/102225/103142/london_underground/>, accessed 1 September 2011. There is no single figure for London bus drivers, who are subject to different pay schemes run by a host of different operators. My best estimate is that a typical bus worker earns an average of £400–£500 per week, 'Bus workers walk out over pay freeze', *East London Lines*, 12 November 2009.

Index